To [...]
appreciation from
Mike & Noela Miller

We wish you tons
of happy fishing!

The Perfect Life

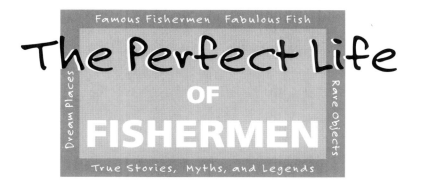

Famous Fishermen   Fabulous Fish

Dream Places

OF

FISHERMEN

Rare Objects

True Stories, Myths, and Legends

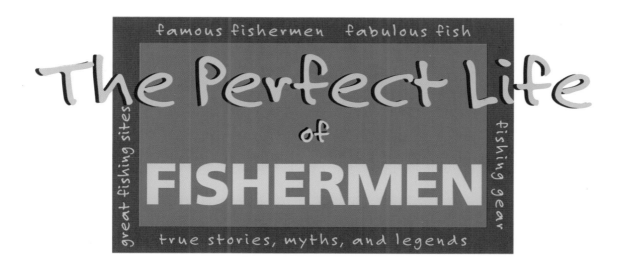

famous fishermen fabulous fish

The Perfect Life

of

FISHERMEN

great fishing sites

fishing gear

true stories, myths, and legends

Text and photographs

by

Pierre Affre

BARRON'S

THE FISHERMAN'S MUSEUM

6

FAMOUS FISHERMEN

20

AROUND THE WORLD

TO YOUR RODS!

la bête noire
C'EST LE FREIN
TROP SERRÉ VOUS CASSEZ
TROP SOUPLE C'EST LA
FUITE IRRÉSISTIBLE
EUL MOULINET
LE
APTA"
progressif
PARTOUT
NEMENTS
Pêches Sportives,
PARIS-IV
SEUL

THE FISHERMAN'S MUSEUM

THE FISHERMAN'S MUSEUM

Mayfly.
Mounting from
the turn of the
century.

The passion for fishing can exist in places far from a body of water. Even if he does not have the soul of a collector, the fisherman is often in love with the beautiful objects that enable him to practice his hobby. It is true that we quickly become attached to the old rod that accompanied us during trips when we came back empty-handed but that also made it possible for us to achieve some fabulous successes. Feeling your fingers around its cork handle, breathing its odor of old varnish, admiring its fine windings, is almost like fishing, even when you are far from the water.

Without being fetishists, many fishermen believe to be infallible the fly or the lure that once enabled them to capture a large number of fish or a record specimen. When they lose it or leave it home and it is not at the end of their line, they will fish without conviction, and obviously, their results will suffer, thus reinforcing their certainty. At the end of their life span, when these lures are chipping, their hooks

bent, broken, or rusty, the fisherman will not throw them away but rather will preserve them religiously, as if they were relics.

Fishing is also practiced in books and in works of art. Like hunting, it is a theme whose first artistic manifestations (sculptures or wall paintings) date back more than thirty thousand years. Many Greek and Roman texts make reference to it, and of course, there are many manuscripts on fishing from the Middle Ages that have been passed down to us today. It is a revealing fact that since the invention of the printing press, the book that has seen the greatest number of printings, after the Bible, is *The Complete Angler* by Izaak Walton. It is very rare that two talents, that of fisherman and that of writer, are united in the same person, as they are in this book. This is a great pity, because the pleasure or the emotion felt upon reading a beautifully written text related to our passion can sometimes equal the sensations experienced when we feel a good catch struggling at the end of our line.

From left to right:
Reels for fishing game fish, tuna, or swordfish. Fly-fishing equipment from the end of the last century.
Ancestor of the spinning reel, a superb Malloch of copper with its line guide.
Rods and reels for fly fishing salmon (start of the century).
Detail of a Hardy rod for game fish, dating from the 1930s.

RODS AND REELS

Although the invention of the fishing rod, an extension of the arm, seems as old as that of the line and the hook, the reel did not appear, at least in Europe, until the 17th century. A simple reserve of line, its sole function at first was to lengthen or shorten the line. In fact, it wasn't until the beginning of the 19th century that it was perfected and made casting possible.

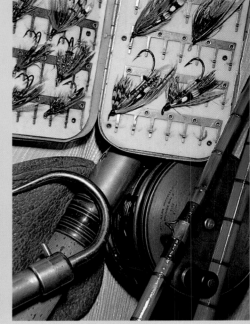

Fishing gear was never more beautiful than at the end of the 19th century.

Modern reels for game fishing are winches mounted with the precision of Swiss watches.

Tackle for salmon fishing, used in the British Isles prior to the First World War.

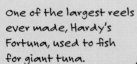

One of the largest reels ever made, Hardy's Fortuna, used to fish for giant tuna.

Before the invention of the open-face spinning reel, only multiplying release reels made it possible to cast lightweight lures.

Bamboo strips (always imported from the southern mountains of China) are planed down to one one-hundredth of a millimeter and glued together to make a fly rod.

Just like beautiful firearms, reels for game fishing may be engraved.

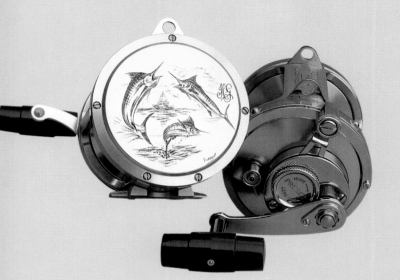

A beautiful Von Hoff reel from the 1930s, the kind Hemingway used.

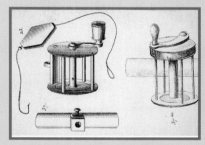

In the 14th century, the line was rudimentary, and the reel did not make its appearance until three centuries later.

A few craftsmen still make unique pieces, such as this splendid titanium fly reel.

was in France, during the 1930s, that the principal improvements to the open-face spinning reel were invented.

Ball bearings and tension adjuster in a Perfect reel dating from the 1920s.

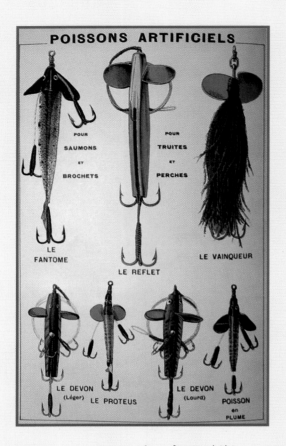

Page from a 1914 Wyers rod and reel catalog. In the era of heavy casting, lures were king.

LURES

In addition to bait, man has tried to deceive fish with lures, imitations of the living prey on which they feed. Lures were first created in bone or wood, but metal and now plastic materials have taken over. The lure is the power of imagination at work.

Swimming fish from Rapala (Finland) imitate all kinds of small fish to perfection.

The "Plucky" movable swimming fish in natural rubber had its hour of glory in the 1950s.

The "terrible," the "formidable," the "devastator": before nuclear submarines, pike had to beware.

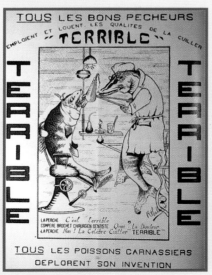

Prior to the invention by Mr. Meulnard of the leaded spinner (the famous Mepps), the lure was for almost half a century the best artificial bait for trout.

This Inuit lure made of petrified walrus tusk is more than a thousand years old.

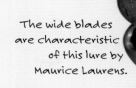

The wide blades are characteristic of this lure by Maurice Laurens.

Lures for trolling made of mother-of-pearl from shellfish, still used by certain tribes in the South Pacific.

The water-witch was one of the first lures imported from England (end of the 19th century).

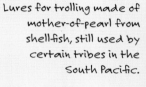

Lures in bone or walrus tusk used for ice fishing by the Naskapis Indians in the Great North, Quebec.

MOUCHES ET INSECTES ARTIFICIELS

From the beginning of the 20th century, the Manufrance catalog offered imitation insects that seemed more real than nature, made of natural rubber.

Invented in the 1930s, the Rublex lure, in natural rubber, produced consistent success for trout and salmon fishermen for more than a quarter of a century.

FLIES

During the first century of the modern era, the Macedonian fisherman who was already deceiving trout with a few cock feathers and silk threads artistically rolled around the shaft of a bronze hook would certainly not have been surprised to find that two thousand years later, artificial fly-fishing is not only an efficient means of bringing home protein, but also a real sublimation of the predatory act.

Real jewels, these Scottish flies for salmon resemble the necklaces of the Xingu Indians of the Amazon.

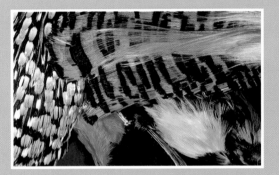

The brilliantly colored feathers of exotic birds were very fashionable in the creation of flies for salmon.

Prewar advertisement for Ragot flies. Today, artificial flies are no longer made in Britain, but in Southeast Asia.

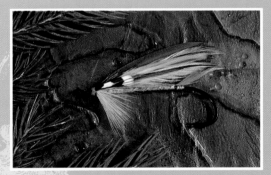

Artificial flies for salmon resemble no known natural prey.

The manufacture of artificial flies for trout calls for the brilliant, vibrant feathers taken from the neck of cocks bred especially for this purpose.

Plate showing flies for salmon taken from a 1932 "Scottish Fisherman" catalog. The collection contains more than three hundred models.

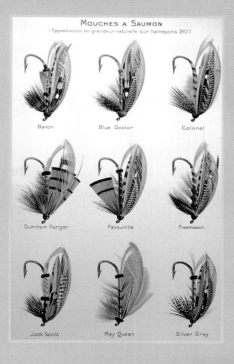

MOUCHES A SAUMON
(Reproduction en grandeur naturelle sur hameçons 2/0)

Baron — Blue Doctor — Colonel
Durnham Ranger — Favourite — Freemason
Jock Scott — May Queen — Silver Grey

To seduce salmon, blues, golds, and oranges mix in a cameo of shades.

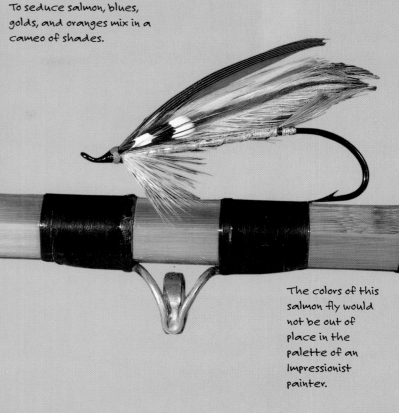

The colors of this salmon fly would not be out of place in the palette of an Impressionist painter.

In the water, the fibers of the various feathers vibrate with the currents and give the impression of being alive.

Halfordian imitation of the *Ephemera danica*, or mayfly.

The wing of this fly made with a jay feather imitates a small alevin on the run.

Trout flies from the 19th century, mounted for use in the hills of Florence.

53

Dyed Gallina

ACCESSORIES

Unlike hunting, fishing has always required a number of small accessories needed for success. These objects often have a magic or sacred character, which makes them even more valuable to the collector.

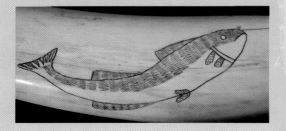

Salmon engraved on a walrus tusk. Detail from an Inuit fish club.

Giant wooden hook, used by the Indian tribes on the west coast of Canada.

What advertising director today would dare to extol the merits of a radioactive product?

Advertising for the Violet Byrrh brand was often based on the theme of sport fishing.

Inuit fish club.

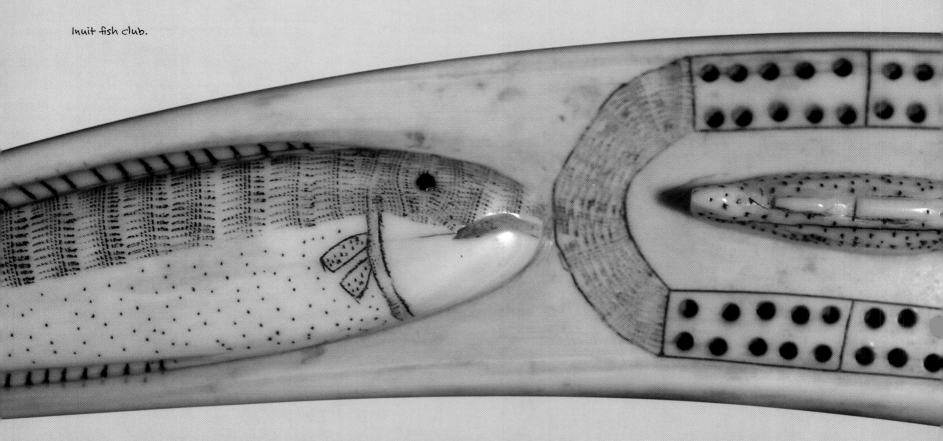

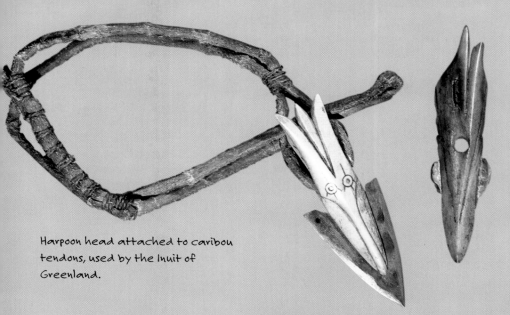

Harpoon head attached to caribou tendons, used by the Inuit of Greenland.

When the beautiful combines with the utilitarian: detail from the head of a harpoon made of walrus ivory.

Slicing through the air like its namesake, the famous Kingfisher natural silk fly line.

Fishing tools from the end of the 16th century differ very little from those used today.

Logo of the Casting Club of France, fashionable organizer of international casting competitions in the 1930s.

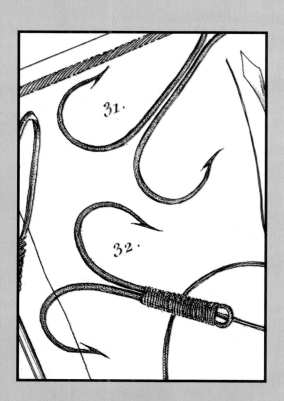

Hooks and ties for fishing pike. Plate excerpted from The French Fisherman, published in 1818.

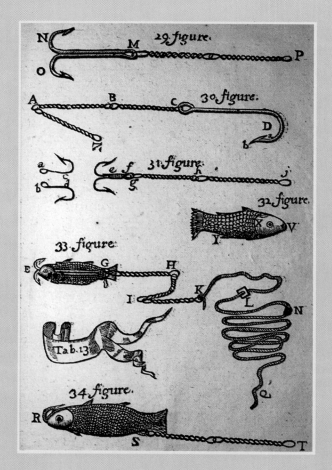

BOOKS AND ENGRAVINGS

La nature & diuerſité des poiſſons,

Auec leurs pourtraicts, repreſentez au plus pres du naturel.

Par Pierre Belon du Mans.

A *Monseigneur le Reuerēndiſſ. Cardinal de Chaſtillon.*

A PARIS.

Chez Charles Eſtienne, Imprimeur ordinaire du Roy.

M. D. L V.

Although Anglo-Saxon literature is rich in works devoted to trout and salmon fishing, the oldest and most beautiful books devoted to the natural history of fish are French. One has only to admire the engravings that illustrate the works of Belon du Mans and Rondelet to be convinced.

Published in 1555, decorated with splendid wood engravings, the book by Pierre Belon du Mans predates by one year that of Guillaume Rondelet.

In the 19th century, fly casting was done with a "lover" or coil. The reel served only to hold extra line.

It was not until the period between the two world wars that fly-fishing with a reel was developed.

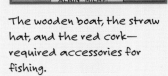

Prior to the invention of nylon (1942), casting lines were made of braided natural silk.

The wooden boat, the straw hat, and the red cork—required accessories for fishing.

With heavy rods made of split bamboo, silks that became sticky, and fragile gut leaders, fly-fishing before the war was not all relaxation.

Since the end of the 19th century, American women have distinguished themselves at catching large game fish.

Fishing for giant tuna off the coast of Nova Scotia.

Splendid wood engraving showing the head of a male salmon (not a female salmon, as labeled) (Belon du Mans, 1555).

DE CYPRINO Cap. XL
SYNONYMA. ETYMVM.

A friend of Rabelais, Guillaume Rondelet gave us an admirable work, The Natural History of Fish.

Excerpted from "Bloch" (1784), these engravings of a brown trout (below) and a river perch (right) have not been equalled since.

For our British cousins, even the very aristocratic hobby of trout fishing was not viewed without humor.

From Egyptian, Greek, or Roman antiquity until almost the end of the Middle Ages, the techniques for line fishing remained practically unchanged.

19

FAMOUS FISHERMEN

FAMOUS FISHERMEN

Although in Latin countries hunting was always celebrated as a worthwhile and even elitist activity, as much for the nobility as it was, later, for politicians or captains of industry, fishing often had a rather pejorative image.

The caricaturists of the 19th and early 20th century devoted themselves to it with great joy, Daumier in the lead, and the figure of the fat gentleman seated on a camp stool and dozing following a good meal accompanied by wine, immobilized for good, is, unfortunately, still connected with our sport. Known as the sport of idlers, poets, dreamers, nonvoters, or the economically weak, fishing has never had a very positive image in France. This is certainly because of the fact that few of its famous countrymen publicly claim their membership in the brotherhood of those who carry fishing rods and landing nets. In contrast are the Anglo-Saxon and Scandinavian countries, where the practice of fishing carries a connotation that is very chic, even snobbish, and crowned heads, presidents, ministers, rich industrialists, and bankers are fervent practitioners.

It would take too much space to list them all here, but let us remember that Presidents Theodore Roosevelt, Dwight David Eisenhower, Jimmy Carter, and more recently, George Bush, made fishing, ahead of golf, their preferred sport. In England, the Queen Mother and Prince Charles are fervent fans of fishing for salmon, the royal fish. The kings and princes of Denmark and Norway are highly skilled. Among business celebrities, Rockefeller and Howard Hughes and, today, Ted Turner and Bill Gates were or are passionate fly fishermen. Among writers, there is Ernest Hemingway, of course, but today Jim Harrison and Thomas McGuane are fans of fly-fishing. In Hollywood, Gary Cooper, Robert Redford, Harrison Ford, and Sean Connery have been fans of trout or salmon fishing. All we have to do is share their passion.

From left to right:
In the 19th century, fishing as a hobby was reserved for the well-to-do.
Billy Pate, probably the most complete fly fisherman in the world.
Since the end of the Second World War, light casting has democratized the sport of fishing.
Hemingway, with a small circle of admirers at Finca Vingi in Cuba.
Anonymous fishermen from the turn of the century.
Mrs. Farrington (friend of Hemingway) and one of her many records.

STUDY TO BE QUIET

A beautiful stained glass window from Winchester Cathedral is dedicated to the memory of Izaak Walton, meditating on the banks of the Dove.

The equipment used in the 17th century is described in detailed fashion in Izaak Walton's book.

Title page from the first edition of *The Complete Angler*, published by Marriot in 1653 (Fleet Street, London).

For Izaak Walton, fishing was a good sport to do or share with friends.

Fisherman as he might have been imagined more than three centuries ago on the banks of the Dove or the Itchen.

Izaak Walton: the complete angler

The *Complete Angler* is very contemplative and filled with rural poetry; who would believe that this book, so innocent and charming, was written during one of the most disturbed and violent periods in the history of England?

As Léonce de Boisset wrote, "By a singular irony of fate, Izaak Walton, whose name will be handed down to posterity as that of the model of the smiling philosopher, a lover of peace and quiet, born during the end of the reign of the Tudors, would grow up and live his long life under the first Stuarts, one of the most violent periods in the history of England. In this period, old Raleigh, the all-powerful Stratford, and many others would put their heads on the block in the Tower of London, the seductive Buckingham would be murdered, Walton's country would be ravaged by two civil wars and devastated by the plague, his house burned during the Great Fire, and the head of his king would fall under the executioner's ax." *The Complete Angler* was first published in 1653, and the immediate success of the work obliged Walton, up until 1676,

Portrait of Izaak Walton on the frontispiece of the third edition of *The Complete Angler.*

In his book, Walton devotes much time to describing fishing for trout using natural bait.

The Complete Angler

THE COMPLETE ANGLER AT WORK
Izaak Walton

"Because these poor scoffers, we fishermen feel enormous commiseration for them and we do not need to borrow their thoughts to believe that we are completely happy. As for the fisherman's simplicity of mind, if by that you mean an innocence of spirit, a simplicity such as was found among the first Christians, who were like the fishermen of today, calm and peaceful individuals so ingenuously wise that they would not sell their consciences to buy riches and, with riches, worries and fear of dying, if you mean simple beings such as lived during the times when there were fewer men of the law than there are now, then we are happy, my colleagues and I, to be considered as such."

"The book is written in the form of a lively dialogue between a hunter, a falconer, and a fisherman . . ."

to devote himself to various successive editions of the book, considerably revised, corrected, and expanded (there were five editions during the author's lifetime). With the exception of the Bible, *The Complete Angler* has been reissued the greatest number of times since Gutenberg invented the printing press. In 1975, there were more than four hundred different editions of the book in the English language alone. The book is written in the form of a lively dialogue between a hunter, a falconer, and a fisherman discussing the various merits of their respective arts. It is divided into twenty-one chapters dealing with different species of fish, accompanied by philosophical digressions as well as magnificent poems. Songs are even included to liven up the chapters that the author probably considered too technical. Finally, what seems most astonishing in an English-language book is that the catching of each fish is followed by an appropriate recipe that even the greatest French chefs would have appreciated.

Izaak Walton's house on Fleet Street, London, was completely reduced to ashes in the Great Fire of 1666.

Meditation and tranquility were inseparable, for Walton, from a day spent on the banks of a river.

The Complete Angler

THE COMPLETE ANGLER AT WORK
Izaak Walton

"And later, an intelligent fisherman can stroll on the banks of the river and identify what kinds of flies are dropping onto the water that particular day, and he will capture some if he sees trout coming up for this type of fly. And then, since he always has prepared fish hooks with him and a game bag containing hair from a bear or heifer that is brown or some other melancholy color, feathers from a cock or a capon, many skeins of colored silk or wool for making the body of the fly, feathers from the head of a duck, black or brown sheep's wool, boar bristles, gold and silver wire, he must also have colored feathers either from small birds, or speckled fowl, I declare that if he has all these items in his game bag and if he can make his fly under good conditions, he will catch so many trout that it will encourage him to become more and more enamored of the art of making flies."

English manor from the 17th century in Hampshire, where Walton frequented the rivers.

After the Revolution and throughout the 19th century, fishing was the favorite pastime of the middle class.

This plate shows the ends of line and leaders made of guitar string, as well as hooks that once were used to fish for pike.

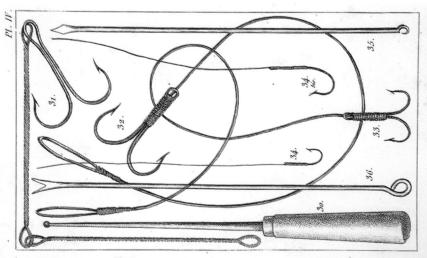

Salmon fly described in *The French Fisherman*, published in 1818, and probably copied from English models of the time.

Good Old Kresz: the French angler

Portrait of Kresz as it appeared in the second edition of *The French Angler*.

During particularly disturbed times in the history of France, first in full revolutionary torment, then throughout the long Napoleonic wars, a young man in his twenties, escaping from the draft, rewarded himself by fishing almost every day. He even found the time to write a well-documented work on the subject titled *The French Angler*.

"It is the first book in French that mentions the invention and use of the reel, . . . "

The similarity with Izaak Walton, who wrote his *Complete Angler* during one of the most tragic periods in English history, is interesting on more than one level, and Kresz can legitimately be considered the French Walton. His book, published for the first time in 1818, must be considered the first modern work in the French language that deals with fishing. It is the first book in French that mentions the invention and use of the reel, describes the equipment in detail, and gives a great deal of advice, some of which still holds true. More than a century and a half before it was to become the fashion, he brilliantly describes the technique of manipulating the bait:

"I went to Neuilly-sur-Marne, three leagues from Paris, toward the end of October 1818. It was almost ten o'clock in the morning when I arrived. My young student was impatiently waiting for me. I told him, toss in your bait, this beautiful gudgeon will be good, beyond this patch of grass, and let it drop to the bottom, bring it back up until it is close to the surface of the water, then let it drop again . . . Bring it up again . . . pull a little to the right and to the left . . . let it sink again . . . bring it up gently . . . stand back a little and bring the bait back to the shore. No bites? Do not lose patience . . . Toss the bait farther and begin again to move it up and down."

"No bites? Do not lose patience . . . "

The success of his book does not seem unwarranted, even after his death, since a sixth, seventh, and even an eighth edition were published in 1861, 1866, and 1868, making *The French Angler* one of the most frequently reissued books on fishing.

A fly-fishing lesson at the time of the Restoration.

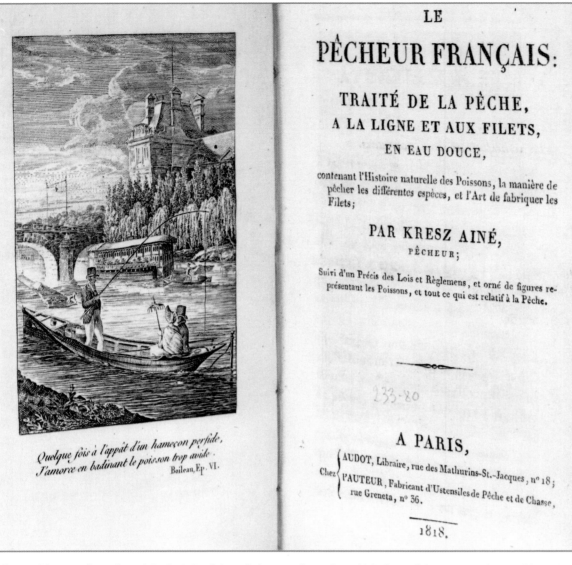

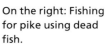

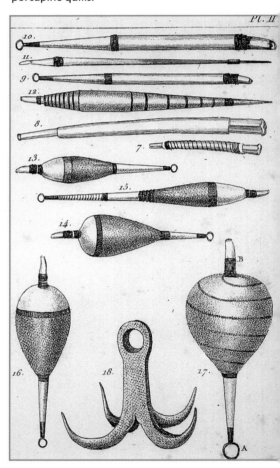

Above: Title page from the original 1818 edition of *The French Angler*, which shows fishermen on the small branch of the Ile de la Cité.

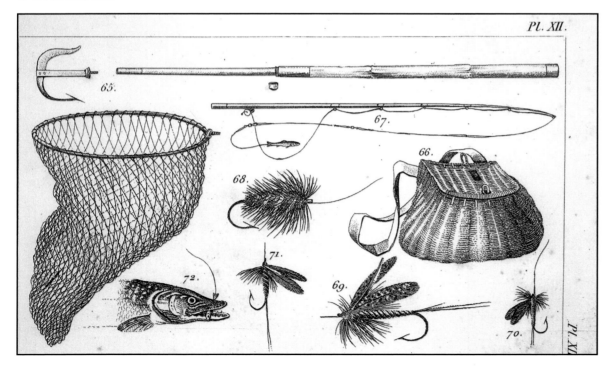

These models of 19th century trout flies actually differ very little from ones used today.

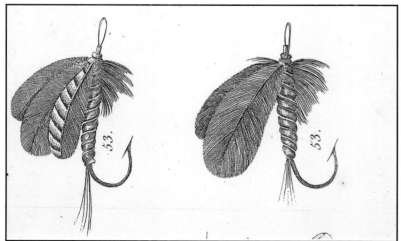

On the left, salmon flies decribed by Kresz.

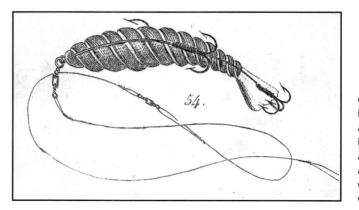

Opposite: The "devil-killer," ancestor of artificial lures. The body consisted of silk and silver thread rolled and tied around a lead weight, finished off with a leather tail.

For the purposes of the dust jacket for his book, *A Fly Fisher's Life*, a room in the Ritz Hotel was transformed into a fishing cabana.

Technical adviser for Pezon and Michel, he tests (successfully) in the United States a new model of open-face spinning reel.

1917: On leave from the U.S. Army, Charles Ritz fishing for pike in the Adirondacks, in northern New York.

Charles C. Ritz: a genial inventor

Badge of the International Fario Club.

At eighty years of age, with a style of absolute purity, Mr. Charles tests his latest invention, the "Vario-Power" of Pezon and Michel.

Charles Ritz completed his education in hostelry, as well as in fishing, in New York, more precisely at the Ritz Carlton, where his father had sent him in 1916. Upon his father's death in 1928, he returned to France to take charge of the most fashionable hotel in the world, the Ritz on the Place Vendôme, opened in 1898.

". . . Ritz was a fantastic angler."

Trained in the school of Fred Payne, the magician of the American rod, he quickly realized that the British-made rods used at the time by French fly fishermen were too heavy and tiring for the hand. Whether it was on the shores of the Risle or in the forests of Boulogne during one of the casting competitions so in vogue during the period between the two wars, he advocated the use of lightweight rods, short and responsive, based on the model he had encountered in the United States. In 1930, 1931, and 1933, he was the French fly-casting champion and proved that with a rod of less than 3.5 ounces (100 grams), it was possible to cast more than 33 yards (30 meters). In 1937, he became the technical adviser to Pezon and Michel, whose worldwide reputation in fishing equipment was matched only by Hardy. In 1938, he created the first Parabolic rod.

Dabbler of genius, Charles Ritz is also the father of the fantastic Telebolic casting rods and, of course, after the war, of the fantastic PPP series. Although he was an inventor and technician of genius, a natural and talented caster, Ritz was also a fantastic angler. Norman trout, Austrian graylings and Norwegian salmon were specialties. His friend Ernest "Papa" Hemingway, who in August of 1945, machine gun in hand, claimed to have liberated the bar at the Ritz, wrote in the preface to the first edition of *A Fly Fisher's Life* by Charles Ritz: "In today's world, very few people have the opportunity to fish as much as Mr. Charles. And even if they did, they would not fish as well as he does."

In 1954, at the weighing crossbar of the Havana Fishing Club, Papa and his faithful skipper, Gregorio Fuentes, show a record wahoo weighing 82 pounds and a small white marlin captured while trolling in the Gulf Stream.

Sailfish

Ernest Hemingway: fist, on the line!

On board the *Pilar*, during the 1950s, with a blue marlin weighing approximately 400 pounds.

"**T**here was an old man who fished alone in a skiff in the Gulf Stream." Thus begins the most beautiful fishing story ever written.

"But it was also the famous author's swan song..."

Although the New York critics had for several years raged against him and said he was finished as a writer, Hemingway refuted them in the most scathing manner by publishing in a 1952 issue of *Life* magazine the first chapters of *The Old Man and the Sea*. Throughout the United States, newsstands were sold out, and a reprinting was necessary. The book was and remains, a half-century later, one of the greatest literary successes of all time, earning for its author the Pulitzer Prize, followed by the Nobel Prize for literature the following year. But it was also the famous author's swan song and the last great work Ernest Hemingway published in his lifetime.

It was in Key West that Hemingway's passion for game fishing was born. His friend the novelist John Dos Passos had persuaded him in 1926 to come and visit him in this large fishing village of great colonial charm. Hemingway had begun to be known, thanks to the appearance one year earlier of his book *The Sun Also Rises*, which had been an instant success. He immediately adored Key West. Dos Passos helped him catch his first sailfish and his first tarpon, and two years later, with the money from *A Farewell to Arms* published in 1929, Hemingway bought a magnificent Spanish colonial-style house, which today has been transformed into a museum. Very soon, the sailfish and the tarpon of Florida held no secrets for him. In 1932, he made his first trip to Cuba, crossing the Florida strait in a small boat belonging to Joe Russell, a sometime smuggler and the owner of the famous bar Sloppy Joe's. In Havana, Hemingway discovered the Gulf Stream and the large predators that hunt in its blue waters. These fish—tuna, marlin, and sailfish—would become a real challenge for him.

Game fishing equipment on the ceiling of the *Pilar*'s cabin: Tycoon rods and Hardy and Fin-Nor reels.

On the roof of the *Pilar*'s cabin, Papa searches the blue waters for a sign indicating the presence of a marlin or a sailfish.

Built in the Brooklyn Navy Yard in 1934, the *Pilar* was a formidable "fishing machine."

At the exit to the port of Havana, Hemingway battles a hundred-pound tarpon. Mary, his wife at the time, often accompanied him on board the *Pilar*.

". . . if the latter [the fisherman] simply wants to be proud of his catch, he must bring the fish in by his own efforts . . ."

This was a real sporting challenge, since the equipment of the period did not make it possible, as it does today, for just anyone to fight such adversaries and win.

Moreover, in 1937 he wrote: "The development of game fishing was slowed down for many years by equipment that was not adapted to these large fish. Today, this type of fishing is in the process of becoming totally without interest from the sporting point of view, simply because of the development in recent years of equipment that is too efficient. . . . The equipment available today often finds its reason for being in the very understandable desire of fishing guides who want to take big fish for their clients, while the latter are physically incapable of leading these fish to the gaff in an honest and sportsmanlike manner. . . . Fishermen, when they tell about their battle with a large fish, forget to say that the latter has a hook planted in its jaw, the back of its throat, or its stomach. It seems to me that this is an already sufficient advantage for the fisherman because it is the fish and not he that has the hook in the mouth, and that if the latter simply wants to be proud of his catch, he must bring the fish in by his own efforts, holding the rod and the reel in his hands, or, if this is too difficult, by supporting the weight using a harness placed on the shoulders or the back. Finally, he must not receive any outside

Translated into many languages, *The Old Man and the Sea* is one of those great stories that we grew up with.

Nameplate of Hemingway's boat.

assistance, until the end of the line is brought in by himself and himself alone, within reach of the hand of the guide who is helping him."

We could not be more clear. The ethic of big game fishing was stated and the rules of the game defined, because if there was a place where Papa Hemingway did not like to see cheaters, it was on board a boat or returning from fishing on a pier. In 1937, during a fishing tournament at the Havana Yacht Club, a competitor arrived at the weighing crossbar with a magnificent marlin that weighed about five hundred pounds. Hemingway congratulated the fisherman but noted that the man had not perspired at all. "The suntan lotion on his face was intact," he remarked later. This minor detail, not noted by the other competitors and the organizers, started Papa thinking. He also learned about a competition from his professional Cuban fishermen friends, who informed him that this fish had just been sold for twenty-three dollars to a rich "gringo" whose description corresponded exactly to our man. The next day, this fisherman, who was of course, disqualified, left Havana and was never heard of again in big game fishing circles. Papa hated cheaters.

"Papa hated cheaters."

THE OLD MAN AND THE SEA
Ernest Hemingway

"Slowly, regularly the line came up; suddenly the ocean rose in front of the boat and the fish appeared. It continued to rise, water streaming along its sides; it sparkled in the light; its head and its back were deep purple and the sun fully illuminated its wide lilac stripes. It had a very long nose, as long as a baseball bat, and pointed like a sword. The fish emerged completely, then with the ease of a good swimmer, dove back into the water. The old man had the time to see the large caudal fin in the shape of a scythe sink into the water, then the line began once again to run wild."

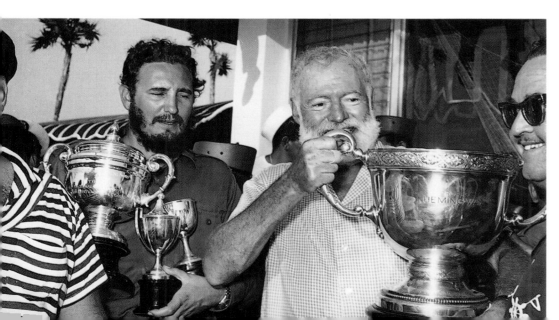

In 1960, at the Hemingway tournament in Havana, Papa presented the winner's cup to the victor of the individual event, Fidel Castro.

Billy Pate is a gentleman, always willing to help or to advise another fly fisherman.

Off the coast of Sherbro, in Sierra Leone, in pursuit of giant tarpon.

Great care is used in the preparation of his equipment. The hook of his gaff is made of titanium alloy.

Off the coast of Quepos, in Costa Rica, Billy battles a hundred-pound sailfish.

During a battle with a tarpon or a marlin, which may last more than six hours, Billy Pate uses golf gloves to keep the Dacron from cutting his fingers.

Billy Pate: fishing for records

This small white marlin, caught by his wife, Jodi, off of Casablanca, is about to be released.

Nothing, at first, would seem to predispose young William Pate, Jr. to becoming the greatest saltwater fly fisherman of all time. Billy, in fact, was born in the Blue Mountains, far from the ocean.

As an adolescent, he assiduously practiced two sports in which he very rapidly excelled: skeet shooting and waterskiing. At the age of fourteen, he joined the American national waterskiing team and participated for some ten years in hundreds of competitions. At the same time, he became one of the best shots in the country in skeet shooting, and quite naturally, he turned to hunting. But before he was even thirty years of age, doctors made him give up shooting because of hearing problems. He thus decided to switch to fishing.

No one has done fly-fishing in as many countries, for so many different species. Although Billy is known above all for his exploits at sea, either fishing for tarpon or rostra (sailfish, marlins . . .), he is also one of the best fishermen for trout and salmon in the world. From Iceland to Tierra del Fuego, from the Rocky Mountains to the tropical jungles of Asia and Central America, there are few places where he has not cast a fly. He was the first and for a long time the only fisherman in the world to have caught the five species of marlin using fly-fishing equipment: white marlin in Venezuela, striped marlin in Mexico, black marlin in Australia, Atlantic blue marlin in Cuba, and Pacific blue in Costa Rica. But the fish that made him famous is the *silver king*, as the tarpon is known in Florida. He fished this species for more than thirty years, an average of a hundred days per year, and held most of the world records. Many times he battled with giant tarpons for more than ten hours, and once even for thirteen hours, only to lose them at nightfall, at the end of his strength and running out of gas. His current world record fish of 188 pounds was vanquished quickly, in less than thirty minutes.

"Many times he battled with giant tarpons for more than ten hours . . ."

The reels that he used are considered by most specialists to be the most reliable for saltwater fly-fishing.

His fingers straining on the handle and the line, Billy makes the fish work hard.

AROUND THE WORLD

AROUND THE WORLD

From the peaceful chalkstreams of southern England to the tumultuous rivers of the Andes cordillera, from the mountain streams of the Pyrenees to the rivers of the Gaspé Peninsula in Canada and Karelia in Russia, from the Florida Keys to the tundra of Ungava Bay, the playing field of the modern fisherman has become more global.

The grass is always greener on the other side of the hill, but let us note that European countries, densely populated and industrialized since the mid-19th century, did not always know how to preserve a setting that would permit the practice of our hobby in an idyllic environment. From this point of view, the Anglo-Saxon and Scandinavian countries have succeeded better than those of Latin origin in preserving quality fishing, especially for salmon and carnivorous fish, but it is particularly to the wild, open, natural spaces, whether American, Asian, or African, that we dream of going

Small Scottish grilse.

one day, to cast our flies or our spinners. Trips are less and less expensive, and the destinations offered are infinite and there for the asking. Wherever there is water—fresh, brackish, or salt—there are fish. Trout, salmon, and tarpon and marlins in the ocean, in order to survive, all need pure water and biotopes that change as little as possible. In their pursuit, fishermen will discover untapped areas, far from civilization or at least from uncontrolled urbanization. Trout rivers, whether in Normandy, the Franche-Comté, Russia, or America, flow far from cities, and the citizens that we have become have a periodic need to escape from the concrete and the asphalt to find calmness and serenity along their banks. Happiness is greater in a field when a river runs through it. It is up to us to save these places of nature and liberty, necessary for fish and for humans, to protect them, even to restore them, in order to hand them down to future generations.

From left to right:
Salmon fishing on the Spey, in Scotland.
The Rio Grande in Tierra del Fuego, known for runs of enormous sea trout.
The Kispiox River comes down from the glaciers of the Canadian Rockies.
In Oregon, the Umpqua River is noted for its steelhead trout.
Only a few experienced guides can venture into the rapids of the Dean, in British Columbia.
The crystal waters of Assetmaquagan, in the Gaspé Peninsula.

The Avon in Netheravon, where Frank Sawyer, inventor of clear-water nymphing, held the position of river keeper for more than a half-century.

The Test in Broadlands, property of the late Lord Mountbatten, last viceroy of India. It was here that Prince Charles learned fly-fishing.

The Chalkstreams: the South of England

The Itchen with its cover of green. Since the beginning of the 20th century and according to the rules established by Halford, a fly is cast here only on a fish identified by a rise.

For a dry fly fisherman, the chalkstreams of Hampshire (an area southwest of London) surely represent Mecca, the sanctuary where it is necessary to make at least one pilgrimage in a lifetime to cast a dry fly upstream, to a waiting fish previously identified by its surface feeding.

As early as the beginning of the 17th century, Izaak Walton was interested in the trout that thrived there. Two centuries later, Marryat, certainly the first, cast an artificial fly almost the way we do now and not with a flywheel, as had been practiced until that time. But of course, it was Halford, a few years later, who codified the rules according to a very strict etiquette for fly-fishing using only a dry fly, and still cast necessarily upstream.

As bucolic and natural as they seem, however, its streams are in fact artificial and date only from the 16th century. It was Dutch engineers who, at the request of Hampshire sheep breeders (the wool industry was at its apogee in England), transformed the enormous unhealthful swamps of the region of Salisbury into what we know today. Canals

The chalky rivers of southern England are the site of fabulous hatchings of large mayflies every year, from May until the beginning of July.

Above, the peaceful feeding of a brown trout in the Test indicates that the long-awaited hatching has begun.

To the right, artificial flies from the 19th century (pre-Halfordian period), used as wet flies.

A pair of trout.

An imitation of a mayfly (*Ephemera danica*) pulled this beautiful wild trout from the Itchen.

were dug, sluice gates installed, and the branches of the river drawn, assuring both drainage for the rich pasture land and the possibility of flooding it instantly in summer to always have fresh and tender grass. Not only have the Test, Itchen, Avon, Kennet, and the other chalkstreams of Hampshire never known the least pollution, but these bodies of water, taking into account their symbolic, historic, and economic importance, are always maintained with the same attentive care that was given at the end of the 19th century. And 1- to 3-pound trout that suck in the small *Baetis* there are the worthy descendants of the brown trout that rejected the imitations presented by Halford himself.

In a dark, rocky cave, at the bottom of a wooded cirque, flows the Loue, the reappearance of the Doubs, that cascades down the splendid gorges of Noailles.

A striped trout from the Loue. Wild trout, native to the area, have, like their relatives in the waters of Franche-Comté and tributaries of the Rhone drainage area, the characteristic coloration of the Mediterranean trout.

The Franche-Comté: Courbet's trout

In matters of fly-fishing for trout and grayling, the Loue and the upper Doubs are certainly the only French rivers that can compare with the most beautiful sites in Bavaria, Austria, or Slovenia.

The residents of Franche-Comté even claim that the Loue is the most beautiful river in the world. It is possible that they exaggerate, but none of the fishermen who have traveled along the banks of these streams between Cléron and Chenecey-Buillon have been able to refute them. The Loue of the Noailles gorges, that of Miroir de Scey, the Loue of the flats and the aprons that follow one another between Mouthiers and Ornans is actually one of the last French rivers to resist the perverse effects of progress and the dubious talent of urban planners. Flowing out of view of indiscreet glances and far from the road, at the foot of breathtaking limestone cliffs where the last peregrine falcons in France take refuge, it is, in addition, jealously protected by a handful of rural owners who have for a very long time been conscious of the tourist and fishing value of their property.

". . . It is still possible to see giant trout lying in ambush in the grass and schools of more than a hundred large graylings in a gravel pit."

Just as before the war, when Charles Ritz and Tony Burnand held sway there, it is still possible to see giant trout lying in ambush in the grass and schools of more than a hundred large graylings in a gravel pit. Fishing is more difficult today than it was long ago, but coming up empty-handed in the mid- or upper Loue is never caused by a lack of fish. Simply, the brown trout of Vuillafans or Chenecey-Buillon, the graylings of la Piquette or Sanso have seen so many flies of so many different types pass by that they don't allow themselves to be fooled so easily. Perhaps even more secret than the Loue, the Cuzancin and the Dessoubre are two other splendid examples of karstic reappearance. And what shall we say about the upper Doubs, near Goumois, on the Franco-Swiss border, where the Mediterranean trout, the striped trout, are probably the most difficult in the world to fool? It is no surprise that the greatest names in fly-fishing meet at Moulin du Plain every year to see if they have kept up their skills.

In the mid-Loue, the famous twists and turns of la Piquette, seen from high on the limestone cliffs that overhang the left bank.

These two enormous wild trout, 15 pounds in all, were caught by nymphing on a public stretch of the Loue.

Above: As the upper Loue passes through the village of Lods, the old barrages of the royal foundries mix and oxygenate its water.

Opposite: Downstream from Ornans, the Loue enters a narrow valley that is difficult to access. It conceals some of the most beautiful "fly-fishing" sites in all of Europe.

The banks of tufts, limestone concretions that form natural barriers across rivers, have a role in the oxygenation of the water and are hiding places for large trout.

At Lynn, a few miles downstream from Balmoral, the Dee enters a narrow, rocky path that salmon and sea trout must cross to reach the clearings upstream.

On the Dee, as on many Highland rivers, opening day in March has often taken place in the snow.

At Craighellachie, a village famous for its distilleries, the Spey offers one of the most beautiful sites for salmon fly-fishing in the world.

Scotland: peaceful rivers and tumultuous gorges

For the entire 19th century and the first half of the 20th, England was becoming overly industrialized and its rivers paid a heavy price for the barriers, the factories, and their procession of pollutants. Scotland, a country of sparsely populated highlands, remained, with the exception of the region around Glasgow, removed from industrial and urban progress.

" . . . a country of sparsely populated highlands . . . "

What at the time might have seemed like a handicap for development quickly proved to be, in the beginning of the second half of the 20th century, an enormous tourist attraction, which the Scots have known how to exploit to the maximum. Scotland today is of course kilts, tweed, cashmere, whiskey, castles, bagpipes, folkloric festivals, and the welcome of its inhabitants, but it is also a veritable paradise for fishing and hunting. An intelligent agricultural system, focused primarily on breeding livestock and very respectful of ecological balances, has only slightly modified the splendid landscapes that may be discovered by

Tradition and equipment dating from the 19th century for taking a salmon with a fly.

The Dee River in Aboyne. For salmon fly-fishing, the rivers of the Highlands offer ideal waters. Large rods, held with both hands, are still frequently used in Scotland.

The Highlands of Scotland, kingdom of the stag, the trout, and salmon.

This small "springer" weighing about 10 pounds, caught on the Dee, will be released.

On the Tay, fishing is done from on board large boats, by trolling a fly or lure across the currents.

Classic salmon flies, "fully dressed" like this Silver Doctor, are widely used on the rivers of Scotland.

To the right: A Hardy rod, with a line of natural silk and a copper reel dating from the 19th century, the ne plus ultra for taking a beautiful spring salmon.

". . . the salmon were so numerous that at ten o'clock in the morning we had to stop fishing . . ."

". . . it is possible to fish for salmon with a small hand rod . . ."

chance along the small roads winding their way along rivers where trout and salmon abound.

This is not by chance, since almost all of the good flies to be used with salmon and sea trout were invented in Scotland. Jock Scott, Green Highlander, Lady Caroline, Mar Lodge . . . Throughout the entire world, from Quebec to Norway and from Iceland to the Pyrenees, these names are synonymous with sure value for salmon fishermen. And if in other countries fishing for *Salmo salar*, in terms of the number and weight of catches, seems better than in Scotland, it will never be that perfect or take its place. It is an immense pleasure to be guided by an old *ghillie** all dressed in tweed, on a path to the Spey, the Dee, or the Tay, and to hear told, in the rolling *r*'s of stories of past times, that the salmon were so numerous, that at ten o'clock in the morning, we had to stop fishing, because six was the maximum number of fish that could be reasonably transported on a bicycle. Just as a trout fisherman should have, at least once, cast a small BWO (Blue Winged Olive) upstream on an apron of the Test or the Itchen, it is necessary to have cast one's line on a great current of a Highlands river to appreciate all of the history behind salmon fly-fishing.

In Scotland, there are several hundred rivers for sea trout and salmon. From the small coastal rivers of Caithness and Sutherland, which can be crossed in three long strides on blocks of stone without getting the feet wet, to powerful Highlands rivers, the choice is broad. Some travel by meandering peacefully in a landscape of heather moors, whereas others clear a passage as they roar through harrowing gorges. On many rivers in the north and on the west coast, it is possible to fish for salmon with a small hand rod, exactly as we would for trout in large streams. On the other hand, for fans of wading and long casts with a 15- or 16-foot rod, the large pools of the mid- or lower Spey, or the powerful currents of the Tay have few equals in the world. A unique trait among the countries that succeeded in conserving their stock of salmon, in Scotland it is possible to fish for these fish throughout the

year, from mid-January until mid-December. In the same river, the run of winter salmon begins in December and continues until March, and fishing there often takes place in a landscape reminiscent of winter sports. Beginning in April, and especially in May and until mid-June, the bulk of the schools of spring salmon arrive. Then it is the turn of the *grilses* (small summer salmon weighing an average of 5–6 pounds) and sea trout, large groups of which are brought into pools by each tide from the end of June to the end of August. Finally, from September to the beginning of December, the large autumn salmon make their run. These may weigh more than 50 pounds, and castings of them are often found decorating the dining rooms of the castles and manors of the Highlands.

This 18-pounder from the Spey is compensation for hours and hours of casting.

*Ghillie: equerry in Gaelic. He is both a fishing warden and a servant. He carries the rods, attaches the flies, selects them if you should so desire, and shows you the good places to cast.

The Pyrenees: the fly fisherman's paradise

In the crystalline waters of the mountain stream of Ossau, trout abound, but are not easy to fool.

The mountain streams of the Pyrenees were once as famous for salmon fishing as the rivers of Scotland or Norway.

Waiting for the formidable strike, this fisherman from Bearn is watching his fly drift.

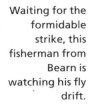

". . . the rivers of the Pyrenees offer pure waters . . ."

At the base of snow-covered mountain peaks, the rivers of the Pyrenees offer pure waters filled with fish in a natural setting that is lush and wild. In the west of the chain, the Bearn and the Basque country are the happy medium between the mountain and the plain, between the blue of the sky and the green of the prairies, between the ocean and the leafy forests.

". . . in a setting that is always grandiose, natural, and changing."

In the center, the High Pyrenees, with torrents cascading in cirques and high-altitude lakes set in the rocks, is the realm of fishermen and hikers. Closer to the ocean, the Pyrenees subside and give rise to a hydrographic network with Mediterranean characteristics. In altitude, the Carlitte massif harbors some of the most beautiful mountain lakes in the chain. Nowhere else in France, or even in Europe, will a sport fisherman find such a large variety of salmonids in the same region. In the Bearn and in the Basque Country, salmon and sea trout live alongside brown trout from mountain rivers and streams. In high-altitude lakes in the central part, char, landlocked salmon, and even lake trout, originally from Canada, abound. Finally, on the Mediterranean side, alongside the southern black trout, you will find the only rainbow trout actually adapted in France. Whether fly-fishing or spin casting, who could ask for more, especially in a setting that is always grandiose, natural, and changing. On the ocean side and in the center of the chain, reserves of mountain snow provide the rivers with an ideal amount of water practically throughout the year, but particularly in July and August, the best months for fly-fishing. Let us add that the waters of the Pyrenees are free of pollution and offer the salmonids conditions that are favorable for their reproduction and growth. For the last twenty years, we must also salute the work undertaken by the managers in the Pyrenees, who have provided ladders and functional fish passes for the barriers that have hampered, often for more than a century, the migration of salmon and sea trout.

Iceland: secret land

The estuary pool on the Laxa I Aadal, immediately downstream from the great falls, is an obligatory stop for salmon that ascend this river.

In the midst of blocks of lava and basalt, this fisherman introduces his fly into the small veins of current containing the salmon.

Iceland is the European country with the fewest varieties of freshwater fish, since only five species live in the cold waters of the island's rivers and lakes.

"...the strongest and most costly demand for tourist fishing in the world."

But, paradox of zoogeography, it is also the country that has experienced the strongest and most costly demand for tourist fishing in the world. It is true that aside from a few eels lost in the Sargasso Sea and brought as far as Reykjavik by a branch of the Gulf Stream, the four other species of fish are those most prized by sport fishermen—the brown trout, the sea trout, the salmon, and the Arctic grayling. Since Reykjavik is only a three-hour plane ride from New York, the North American demand, especially with regard to salmon fishing, is very high, which also explains the often high price demanded for renting a good site. In fact, there are no bad sites in Iceland. All of the rivers on the island, including the one that flows through Reykjavik (120,000 inhabitants), are totally free of pollution

54

It was here in the Hafralónsá that the largest salmon in Iceland was caught in 1998. It weighed 29 pounds.

RIVERS OF ICELAND
Major Stewart

a"We were somewhat at a disadvantage on the Mitfjardara in comparison with the other rivers. In fact, no ghillie was available to show us the river, and specifically the good pools for salmon. We thus discovered them by ourselves, and finally we enormously appreciated the fact that no one had shown us the good locations. What satisfaction when the surprise of a beautiful fish rewarded our decision to fish in one place rather than another. In one week, we took 63 salmon, 20 Arctic graylings, and 8 brown trout."

Arni Baldurson is considered to be a magician by his Icelandic peers. At thirty-four years of age, he has caught more than five thousand salmon.

To the right: Immediately downriver from the Big Laxa Falls (Husavik region) is probably one of the best salmon pools in the entire world.

"...catching more than ten salmon per day per fisherman is not unusual."

and run through sumptuous landscape, much of which has remained unchanged since the Vikings of Erik the Red colonized the island in the 10th century. On the southwest coast, beautiful pastoral valleys are home to some twenty rivers in their niche of green, the most well known of which are the Nordura, the Grimsa, the Langa, and the Thvera. These rivers, because of their proximity to the Gulf Stream, are the best ones and the salmon begin their run there beginning in mid-June. They often appear in closed ranks, and during the month of July, catching more than ten salmon per day per fisherman is not unusual. Unfortunately, these are not large fish, the majority being *grilses* (salmon that have spent only one year in the ocean) that weigh approximately 6 pounds. On the other hand, on the northern and northeastern coasts, the salmon are somewhat less numerous, but much larger. The climate is more harsh, and the rivers cross landscapes that are more rocky and austere. Many of them often have to forge a passage through canyons of basaltic rock and, at twenty-five miles (forty kilometers) from the ocean, an uncrossable waterfall often blocks the return of the salmon. The best rivers for fishing are the Mitfjardara, the Laxa a Asum, the Sela, the Hofsa, the Hafralónsá, the Laxa I Dolum, and the Laxa in Adaldalur. In the Icelandic language, pure 10th century Norwegian, a river is designated by the addition of the suffix *ó* (pronounced "ao") to a word. Thus, *hafralón* means "lake," and Hafralónsá means "the river that comes out of a lake." But if you take a look on a map of Iceland, you will be surprised by the number of rivers called Laxa (a word generally followed by the indication of the closest known place). There is a good reason for this: *lax* in Icelandic means "salmon," and *laxa* always indicates a river

particularly rich in salmon. But it is not only the salmon that make Iceland worth the detour. In the Myvatn region (geyser park), the Big Laxa, in its upstream portion, is one of the best rivers for large brown trout in the world. Because of the numerous sources of warm water that pour into the river, even in the dead of winter, the larvae of insects, and specifically of aquatic invertebrates, swarm and constitute a tremendous source of food for the trout, which reach record weights in only a few years. Finally, on the southern coast, around Vatnajokull, the second-largest glacier in the world after that of Greenland, there are rivers full of large sea trout and migratory Arctic graylings.

The management of salmon and trout fishing in Iceland is a model of its kind, considering the important economic contributions of fishing tourism for this small country. All of the rivers are "followed" from a scientific point of view, and fishing also is closely monitored. Poaching is virtually nonexistent, and no commercial fishing is authorized in the estuaries or in the area adjoining the coast.

"...the rivers cross through the most austere and rocky landscape."

The Laxa I Dolum carves a passage through the lava flows that bar its route.

At the time of their annual migration, thousands of caribou have to swim across the rivers of Quebec's Great North. Here, Caniapiscau River.

This lake trout of about 5 pounds took a small wobbling spoon.

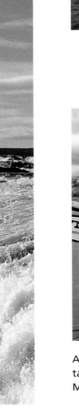

The Georges River tumbles down the Helene Falls in an imposing cauldron of foam on its way to Ungava Bay. This fisherman can expect to catch a salmon, an Arctic char, or a brown trout.

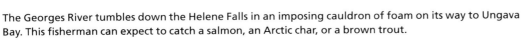

A nice catch of Arctic char taken at Camp Tuktu on Mistinibi Lake.

Quebec and Labrador: immense fishing areas

F or more than three hours, at less than 900 feet (300 meters) of altitude, we fly over hundreds and hundreds of lakes and rivers that wind through the middle of the tundra and where, it is certain, no "Mepps" has ever troubled the tranquility of the inhabitants.

The lakes of Labrador are loaded with Arctic graylings, close relatives of the graylings found in Europe's great Alpine lakes.

". . . hundreds and hundreds of lakes and rivers . . ."

Fighting against a rather strong head wind, little Beaver, slowed down by its enormous hydroplane floaters, does not move very quickly, and we have lots of time to examine the countryside, the herds of caribou in full migration, and even the Canada geese. Little by little the forests of spruce thin out to give way to mosses and lichens, proof that we are arriving at the end of our voyage, the Helene Falls, on the Georges River, not far from Ungava Bay. We took off from Schefferville, a former mining town now closed down, more than 600 miles (1,000 kilometers) north of Montreal. Beyond Ungava Bay, there are Baffin

The hydroplane is the only means of access to the lakes and rivers of the Great North in Quebec.

The immense Canadian expanses offer several thousand miles of as yet unexploited river.

Naskapi tents, quick to pitch and very comfortable.

"This is an enormous country, with natural resources for the most part unexploited . . ."

This 15-pound lake trout took a wet fly intended for landlocked salmon.

Island, one of the most inhospitable places on the planet, and the glacial Arctic Ocean.

The territories of New Quebec and Labrador, almost four times larger than France, are practically uninhabited. Only a few thousand Inuit (Eskimos) and Indians from the Great North (Montagnais and Naskapis) share the animal resources. In summer, some twenty "suppliers" (hunting and fishing organizers) exploit a few chunks of the territory, basically for hunting caribou and fishing salmon, northern pike, and *touladi* (the Indian name for lake trout). This is an enormous country, with natural resources for the most part unexploited and unknown to even the majority of people in Quebec. It is true that in a radius a few hundred miles north of Montreal or Quebec, there are so many lakes and rivers with speckled trout, brolon trout, graylings, Canadian pike and lake salmon, that the inhabitants have no reason to lose themselves in the territories of New Quebec, accessible only by hydroplane. At the very top, the Feuilles River, the Mélèzes River, the Caniapiscau, the Koksoak, and the Georges River are real rivers with dangerous runs, cut by falls and churning rapids,

To the left: The Schiste Falls bar the Caniapiscau River for more than a thousand yards (a kilometer) across.

The clearly forked caudal fin of the lake trout affirms the swimming power of this fish, which can reach weights of 30 to 40 pounds.

A rainbow trout and a lake trout.

where only good guides know how to manage the boats to lead you to spots full of fish.

But Quebec is also the Gaspé Peninsula and the northern coast of Saint Lawrence, areas that are home to some of the best rivers for salmon in the entire world. Restigouche, Matapédia, Cascapédia, Bonaventure, Saint-Jean, Moisie, Saint Anne, the river of the Wolves, Saint Marguerite—the names of all these rivers remind us that before being booted out by the redcoats, Jacques Cartier and his sailors were the first to discover them. In these sublime rivers, that were for more than a century (from 1870 to the early 1980s) privatized for the benefit of rich captains of industry and financial magnates from New York, Philadelphia, and Boston, and where, it seems, it was more difficult to obtain an invitation to fish than to be elected to Congress, it is possible today to fish in a more "democratic" manner. The Quebec Fish and Game Department has, over the last twenty years, "de-clubbed" most of these rivers, that is, they have bought back the fishing rights from the rich Americans who held them.

A system of lotteries and day passes has been put into effect, making it possible, today, for tourist fishermen to have access to these mythical rivers where large salmon come to catch their dinner, while you make your flies dance on the smooth surface of the pools. And if you are lucky enough to catch one with your 9-foot rod, perhaps you will follow a no-kill policy and release the fish so that it may continue its trip to the "sanctuary" upstream where, in the autumn, it will in turn give life in the waters where it was born four or five years before.

". . . the most beautiful salmon rivers in the world."

". . . large salmon come to catch their dinner, while you make your flies dance . . ."

Pure waters that cascade from lake to lake across the barren grounds of the Great North of Quebec.

To the left: In the south of the Kola Peninsula, the Umba meanders through the heart of a forest of pines, alders, and birch.

Kola Peninsula: the salmons of perestroika

A boat is useful, in the powerful waters at the beginning of the season, for fishing in the pools found in the lower portion of the Umba.

I t was only at the end of the 1980s, thanks to perestroika, that Western sport fishermen heard about the fantastic possibilities for Atlantic salmon fishing offered by the rivers of the Kola Peninsula.

"The discovery of this new El Dorado of Atlantic salmon came at just the right time . . ."

This region, bordering on Finland, centered around the military-industrial port of Murmansk, is only about a three-hour flight from Paris or London, but because of the Cold War and ultra-secret nuclear submarine bases, it remained totally closed by the Soviet government for more than half a century. Only a few officers stationed in the camps at the mouth of the various rivers as well as dignitaries and other officials of the regime could boast of having authorization to cast a spinner or a lure there. The first Western fishermen to have the good fortune to be invited could not find enough superlatives to describe the abundance, the record weights, and especially the aggressiveness of Russian salmon toward their flies. The discovery of this new El Dorado of Atlantic salmon came at just the right time, since at the same time the rivers of Scotland, Ireland, and especially Norway were experiencing their most mediocre results since statistics began to be kept more than a century before.

"The only means of access to these rivers is by helicopter . . ."

The rivers of the northern coast of the Kola Peninsula are identical to those in Labrador or northern Iceland, which flow through a rough backdrop of Arctic barren ground. The Litza, the Kharlovka, the Rynda, the Varzina, and the Yokanga work their way, a few miles upstream from their estuaries, through rocky gorges and canyons like the ones on almost all Icelandic rivers. On the Barents Sea coast, past Murmansk, there are no civilian inhabitants, no villages on these rocks that are battered throughout the year by the Arctic winds. At each river mouth is a small military post, with its rusty barracks and spikes of antennas, hiding, perhaps, some nuclear submarine base. The only means of access to these rivers is by helicopter, which depart from Murmansk, weather permitting, and deposit the intrepid fishermen into camps of tents or cabins, generally located on the best pool.

Athletic wading in the Rynda, in the frozen waters of the thaw.

63

Above: On the upper Rynda, Jean-François Gaillard is about to land a magnificent 20-pounder.

At left: Armenian champagne and Polish vodka to accompany the smoked trout of the Kola tundra.

Russians practice fly-fishing with a casting rod and a rudimentary "Buldo" made of wood. Their rustic technique remains very effective.

Nick Podolski, head guide on the Umba, about to release a magnificent freshly caught salmon weighing almost 30 pounds.

The rivers of the southern coast are very different. Accessible by a bad road from Murmansk, they empty into the White Sea and run through a wooded landscape that is reminiscent of the Gaspé Peninsula, intercut with prairies, swamps, and forests of scrub pine. Poor villages of fishermen and lumberjacks exist on almost all the estuaries. The Varzuga, the Pana, the Umba, and the Ponoï are the principal rivers in the south and west of the peninsula. Earlier than those of the northern coast, salmon runs begin in mid-May and continue until the first major snowfalls at the end of October. Although the salmon, except in the Umba, are much smaller on average than those of the Barents Sea coast, they are more numerous, and catches of more than twenty fish per fisherman per day are currently recorded.

The main inconvenience of these rivers: beginning in mid-June and throughout the summer, the salmon are generally small in size, but the mosquitos are gigantic, and unfortunately, far more numerous than the fish. . . .

At the beginning of July, if the winter was rough, there may still be a lot of snow on the banks of the Kharlovka, the pearl of the rivers of the northern coast of the Kola Peninsula.

This double coup, achieved by soldiers "on leave" casting, will perhaps improve the monotony of camp life.

" . . . the salmon from the Barents Sea are probably the most combative in the world . . ."

On the northern coast, because of the permanent icy winds that blow from the Arctic, there are practically no mosquitos, and here it's the salmon that are gigantic. Because of the extreme weather conditions, fishing is dangerous here. In less than an hour, when the winds are blowing, even in July or August, the temperature can drop more than 40 degrees F (15 degrees C) and the fog from the Barents Sea can envelop everything for three or four days, sometimes longer. The rivers are powerful, their rapid, icy currents filled with enormous rocks, and the wading is often dangerous. Yes, it is true, but the salmon from the Barents Sea are probably the most combative in the world and justify by their average weight of 20 pounds and their exceptional fight the high prices demanded for a week of fishing on the Kharlovka or the Litza.

At Pontoon Bridge, an obligatory passing point for salmon and sea trout between the Conn and Cullin lochs.

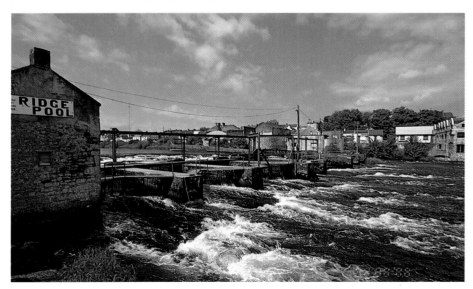

In the heart of the town of Ballina, on the Moy River, is the famous Ridge Pool, where each year hundreds and hundreds of salmon are caught using flies.

François Calmejane, one of the foremost specialists in woodcocks and Irish trout, is shown here, in action on the Clare River, at mayfly time.

Ireland: trout as brown as Guinness

A mild and oceanic climate along with very favorable geology makes Ireland a veritable paradise for fishing for salmonids, pike, and whitefish.

In the western half of the island, enormous outcrops of layers of chalk provide the bottom of lakes and rivers with the best substrata there is for the growth of fish, particularly trout and salmon. The large lakes of Connemara, the Corrib, the Mask, the Conn, and the Cullin, to name only the most well known, have few equals in the world for populations of large wild brown trout.

It is only far away in the Southern hemisphere, in New Zealand or in Argentina, that a fly fisherman will have the opportunity to catch such beautiful fish. Between mid-May and the beginning of June, phenomenal hatchings of large mayflies (*Ephemera danica*) take place on all of these lakes with limestone or chalky bottoms, sending the trout ... and the fishermen ... into a frenzy. Then, during the summer and until the end of September, there will be the hatchings of sedges (phryganes), dozens of species of mayfly, of tipules and other diptera on which they feed. A traditional form of fishing on these large lakes is *dapping*, which consists of allowing oneself to drift with the wind behind while skimming the surface of the waves with a real or artificial fly. But for the sport fisherman, Ireland is also 8,700 miles (14,000 kilometers) of rivers, which for the most part are trout waters, not to mention salmon and sea trout. Whether on the Moy, the Sir, the Blackwater, or the Eriff, salmon and especially the *grilses* (small salmon that return to the rivers in the summer) have returned in force during the last ten years. And here, unlike other countries such as Scotland, Norway, and Iceland, you don't have to be very rich to enjoy good fishing. Since the Irish are not jealous, and since a pint of Guinness has a way of loosening tongues, it is at the local pub that you will easily learn the names of the best places and the fly of the moment.

On the Irish lochs, you will find it easy to rent a boat to fish by *dapping* or trolling.

Splendid specimen of a brown trout, characteristic of the lochs and rivers in western Ireland.

"Catch and release" is not always the rule in Celtic countries; "catch and cook" also has its followers.

Opposite: At the height of summer, the Dean is fed by the melting of glaciers in the Rockies.

Below: The slippery pebbles of the Thompson make wading dangerous.

At left: The Snake, an enormous tributary of the Columbia, at this point marks the border between Idaho and Washington State. Pacific salmon and steelheads ascend for more than 300 miles (500 kilometers).

Above: The tourist fisherman cannot be mistaken: he is in the kingdom of the steelhead.

Opposite: The Thompson River, in southern British Columbia, is known for the aggressiveness of its steelheads.

British Columbia and the Western United States

Between northern California and southern Alaska, on the coasts of Oregon, Washington State, and the Canadian province of British Columbia, the majority of rivers that cascade in falls from the Rockies to empty into the Pacific Ocean experience runs of steelhead trout, which are to rainbow trout what Europe's sea trout are to its brown trout.

". . . access to the best spots requires the rental of a small plane or helicopter."

Just like salmon, these trout spawned in the upstream portions of rivers swim down to the ocean after one or two years to feed, their tour of the feeding grounds carrying them almost as far as Japan. Two or three years later, compelled by the need to reproduce, they return to their native waters, weighing 10 to 20 pounds, capable of handling the most powerful currents.

Unlike Pacific salmon, whose aggressive qualities, once they have returned to freshwater, decline quite rapidly (making fishing outside of the estuaries of little sporting interest), the steelhead, even after a long sojourn in freshwater, retains an aggressiveness and a muscular dynamism that few other salmonids can claim. In Oregon, the Umpqua and Deschutes Rivers, long sections of which are reserved exclusively for fly-fishing, are easily accessible. On the other side of the border, in British Columbia, the rivers in the Vancouver region such as the Fraser and the Thompson can be reached by road, but access to the best spots requires the rental of a small plane or helicopter. The Dean, Babine, and Skeena flow in virgin territory, where encounters with ill-mannered grizzlies are possible. On these rivers, guides organize descents in camping rafts, which make it possible, in one week, to explore the best sections, according to the season and the runs of steelhead.

In crystal water, as here in the Umpqua, steelhead are fished for by sight. Perfect presentation of the fly is necessary to avoid frightening the fish.

Florida Keys: in the wake of Hemingway

In the Keys, fishing marinas can be identified from afar.

THE OLD MAN AND THE SEA
Ernest Hemingway

"He took in the sea with a single glance and realized the infinite solitude in which he found himself. {...} Clouds go to meet the trade winds. In front of the boat, a flock of wild geese cut across the sky; it disappeared, then reappeared, and the old man understood that nothing is ever completely alone at sea."

". . . the blue waters of the Gulf Stream are more than 10,000 feet (3,000 meters) deep . . ."

South of Miami, over approximately 120 miles (200 kilometers), there extends a multitude of islands, big and small, more than five hundred in all, the largest ones linked by bridges to the famous U.S. Route 1, which begins at the Canadian border and ends in Key West, the southernmost city in the United States. Key West is a terminus. You don't pass by Key West, you go there—to have fun, to celebrate the cult of Hemingway, or to fish.

From Miami, U.S. 1 is linked by overpasses to the islands, by means of more than forty bridges, including one seven miles long, and separates the dark blue waters of the Gulf of Mexico and the green waters of the Florida strait, wedged between Cuba and the Bahamas, the place where the Gulf Stream is born.

Nowhere else in the world does there exist such variety and abundance of sport fish: marlins, sailfish, bonefish, permits, barracudas, amberjacks, coryphenes, carangues, and others. On the ocean side, the drop-off is located a few nautical miles off the coast. There, the blue waters of the Gulf Stream are more than 10,000 feet (3,000 meters)

The flats, immense shoals that are uncovered at low tide and extend over millions of acres, from one end to the other of the Florida Keys, are among the most productive biotopes on the planet.

Top right: This tarpon has just come to the surface to take in a lungful of air.
Opposite: In the deepest channels that cut across the mangrove swamp, many sharks lie in wait.

deep and are home to the large majority of pelagic predators: tuna, marlin, swordfish, shark. . . . On the Gulf of Mexico side, there is a complete change of scenery and actors: the flats extend over millions of acres and are visited during each high tide by coastal species that inhabit lagoons and reefs: tarpon, snook, bonefish, carangues. The Florida flats constitute one of the richest ecosystems on the planet. These are muddy, sandy, or chalky shallows, which are uncovered at low tide and which the waves recover four times per day. The back country, as all of the region consisting of the Keys and the end of the Florida peninsula is known, is in fact subject to a double phenomenon of tides, those of the Atlantic alternating with those of the Gulf of Mexico. This is a peculiarity that, to the best of our knowledge, is unique in the world, and the fish as well as the fisherman can take advantage of four movements of water every twenty-four hours. However, in the tropical waters, as elsewhere, the movements of the tide control the passage and appetite of saltwater fish. Fishing, which is done here by sight, using small boats with very shallow draft, is a real hunt.

Off the coast of Key West, the island where Hemingway liked to go to write. His house on piles was swept away by the hurricane that battered the Keys in 1937.

Tierra del Fuego: fishing in the wind!

The gusts of wind are so violent that only the most confirmed fly fishermen can cast their flies.

On the Rio Claro, the vestiges of an underwater forest serve as hiding places for enormous trout, brown and rainbow.

S ixty-two miles (100 kilometers) from Ushuaia, in the rivers that descend from the Andes cordillera and empty into the Atlantic Ocean, run the largest sea trout in the world.

Introduced at the turn of the century by British colonists who had come to raise sheep on the Argentine pampas, trout that originated in Wales and the south of England adapted magnificently to the Southern Hemisphere. The record for a trout caught with a fly on the Rio Grande is currently 35 pounds, or approximately 15.9 kilos. But monsters of more than 44 pounds (20 kilos) have been caught with Rapala. The statistics very meticulously kept since 1982 for a 33-mile (55-kilometer) downstream section of the Rio Grande (Estancia Maria Behety, 173,000 acres) show that more than 80 percent of the fish caught with flies are between 7 and 12 pounds (3 to 5.5 kilos); only 10 percent of the trout weigh less than 6.6 pounds (3 kilos) and 10 percent between 13 and more than 22 pounds (10 kilos).

". . . monsters of more than 44 pounds (20 kilos) have been caught with Rapala."

Fishing is done with fly casting, somewhat like fishing for salmon, or for steelhead in the winter, but here it requires the ability to cast into winds that often exceed 35 miles (60 kilometers) per hour. Don't forget that here we are only a few cables' lengths away from Cape Horn and that there are no trees on the shores of the rivers to break the fury of the southern winds. Even between two gentle breezes, with a background wind blowing at least 25 miles (40 kilometers) per hour, it is futile to try even a minimal back cast before casting the line forward. The fishing technique is one of the most simple, but also one of the most monotonous, descending the pools by methodically combing, or rather, by beating the water with the heavy taper of the deep-diving shooting head. One step downstream, a cast, and so forth, for hours, hoping with each cast that the line will be snatched from your fingers by a giant trout. Then you will forget the wind, the cold, the monotony of the gravel beds, to admire, in its coat of silver scales punctuated with black crosses, one of the most beautiful fish that a fly fisherman has the opportunity to catch.

"One step downstream, a cast, and so forth, for hours . . ."

TO YOUR RODS!

TO YOUR RODS!

From his first trout caught with a worm in a small Norman stream to giant salmon on the Kola Peninsula, from his first bar lost on the pebbles of a small Breton creek to marlin on the Great Barrier Reef, the sport fisherman of today does not hesitate to travel from one continent to another in pursuit of fish that are always bigger, more beautiful, or more aggressive.

The real fisherman is eclectic in the search for his prey, or rather for his adversaries or game partners. To catch a 1-pound trout at the end of an ultra-fine line is not more worthwhile than the taking of a marlin weighing a thousand times that weight. From the explosive fight of a 250-pound (100-kilo) tarpon to the stubborn and sly one of a 20-pound (9-kilo) carp, there is not only the difference in weight, but also in the philosophy of fishing, in the relationship to the fish in question. Of course, the majority of fishermen have a

Salmo vulgaris

Salmo variabilis

Umbla altera

favorite species that they prefer to seek out, with which they familiarize themselves and try to understand all of the wiles, all of the habits, and of course all of the preferences in terms of bait or lures. Others prefer a technique, such as fly-fishing or light casting, which they strive to perfect and to adapt to different varieties of fish. Others are monomaniacs, preferring a single species with a single technique. This is the case with many fly fishermen who are interested exclusively in trout or salmon.

Along with Izaak Walton, we believe, on the contrary, that the perfect fisherman must be interested in all kinds of fish, the most humble and the smallest as well as the largest and most noble, and therefore must master varied techniques to catch them, even if today it is often to release them immediately. There will always be someplace in the world where there is a new fish to discover as well as a new technique to put to use or to invent to make it bite. Boredom in fishing runs no risk of occurring as a result of uniformity.

The first representations of fish, in books of the 16th and 17th centuries (Belon de Mans, Rondelet, Aldrovande, Bonaterre), recall wood, copper, or stone engravings (lithographs).

Salmo ferox

Salmo vulgaris

UMBLA ALTERA

Norbert Morillas, fantastic fisherman from the Franche-Comté, with a wild trout from the Loue weighing almost 9 pounds (4 kilos), caught on 14/100 line.

The Trout: fair lady of our rivers

The word *trout* comes from the Latin *tructa*, which itself is derived from the Greek *troktes*, which may be loosely translated as "voracious." The trout is thus the voracious fish par excellence, that Valenciennes, moreover, did not hesitate to give the scientific name *Falmo ferox* ("ferocious trout").

"The trout is thus the voracious fish par excellence . . ."

Among the numerous scientific names that ichthyologists have given to the trout, *Salmo variabilis* is perhaps the one that most corresponds to reality. Few fish, in fact, demonstrate as many differences in size, coloration, and behavior as the common trout. Blond and fat Norman trout, black and nervous trout from Breton streams, striped trout from the Loue or the Doubs, blue trout from Vivarais, red trout from the Truyère, large spotted trout from Corsica, their coloration so different but always elegant, identifies them as belonging to very specific territories. In general, the back, the sides, and the gill covers are sprinkled with black spots, round or in the shape of a cross, of variable size. The famous red points are not, in fact, always present. And when they exist, they vary in size, are irregular, and are sometimes encircled with blue or cream. The color of the back varies from black to light

Salmo ferox

Salmo ferox

Above: The brown coloration sprinkled with black points and some red spots of these Scottish trout is characteristic of the fish from lochs with peat bottoms.

To the right: The swallowing fish par excellence, the trout takes insects from the surface that are born at the bottom of the river or that fall accidentally from the riverbanks.

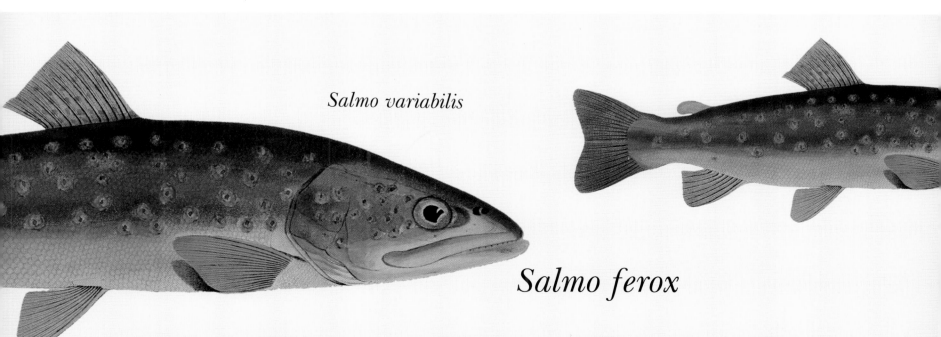

Salmo variabilis

Salmo ferox

Above: Highly pigmented wild trout from the chalky Irish rivers.

To the right: Philippe Boisson, probably the best European specialist in nymph fishing for large wild trout. Here with a prize fish from the Loue.

"The sides may be silver, pearly, golden, or yellowish."

blue, appearing in some strains or "races" as bluish gray or various shades of brown. The sides may be silver, pearly, golden, or yellowish. Finally, the stomach is white, yellow, or perhaps an entire range of mixtures of these two colors. The fins vary from yellow to green, sometimes brown. During the course of hundreds of thousands of years of evolution, each region—and sometimes even each river—has selected varieties or races of trout that have become their own and are perfectly adapted. The nature of the soil, the altitude, the steepness of the water course, the variations in temperature, the kind of food available, and many other factors are responsible for this species' very great polymorphism. Thus, in its fourth or fifth year, a trout from a stream in the Pyrenees or an Alpine torrent won't exceed 6 ounces (150 grams), whereas its Norman cousin will easily reach 3 pounds, not to mention lake trout, which can, at the same age, exceed 22 pounds (10 kilos). But don't let this extreme diversity in size, shape,

These brilliant and lively cock feathers allow just enough light to pass through the fibers to imitate the diaphanous wings of a natural insect.

Almost caught, this trout from the Rio Irigoyen, in Tierra del Fuego, jumps out of the water in an attempt to unhook itself.

to your rods!

Atlantic trout have a coat that is light, pigmented with vermilion.

"... fishermen must combine skill and attentiveness."

and coloration fool you: trout from rivers, streams, and lakes are only what scientists today call the "ecological forms" of the same fish—the common trout. In addition to the elegance of its shape and the beauty of its coat, the trout has as its main attraction for the fisherman the vivacity of its movements, and the discretion of its means of feeding, on the surface in the middle of a small circle, sucking, with a wet sound that sounds like a kiss. To attract them and catch them, fishermen must combine skill and attentiveness. They offer them artificial flies, assemblages of feathers and colored wires artistically rolled around a hook, which are truly small jewels that only distantly resemble the insects on which they feed. However, if they are well presented, with art and style, the trout allow themselves to be lured, perhaps simply because they, too, find them beautiful. In this way, the fisherman may admire them up close, hold them for an instant, and then give them back their freedom.

NATURAL HISTORY OF fiSH
Lacépède

"The trout is not only one of the tastiest fish, it is also one of the most beautiful. Its scales shine with the brilliance of silver and gold; a golden yellow mixed with green shines on the sides of its head and body; the pectoral fins are brown mixed with purple; the ventrals and caudal fin golden; the adipose fin is the color of gold with a brown border, the anal fin purple, gold, and pearl gray; the dorsal fin sprinkled with tiny crimson drops; the back spotted with black spots and other red spots surrounded by a light blue reflecting on the sides of the animal the deep and agreeable shades of ruby and sapphire."

To the left: The grayling is one of the most beautiful of our freshwater fish.

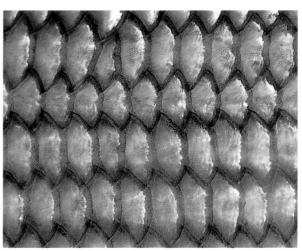

Above and on top: The grayling is caparisoned in large scales, and its dorsal fin, enhanced with purple and crimson blue, is supported by some twenty bony spokes.

The grayling today is classified in the family of thymallides.

The Common Grayling: standard-bearer of the fly fishermen

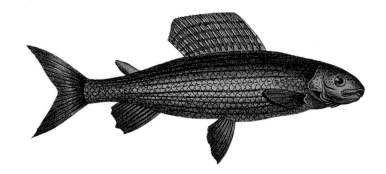

Engraving on wood from the 17th century.

T he European grayling is also known as the umber; this name comes from the Latin word umbra, used for the first time to designate this fish in the poem by Ausone about the Moselle: "When it escapes from view by swimming rapidly, it appears to fishermen more like the shadow of a fish than a real fish."

The grayling prefers water that is pure, fresh but not too cold, flowing moderately over a bottom of gravel or pebbles. It is a gregarious fish, living in schools of a few dozen to more than a hundred individuals. Eclectic in its search for food, it feeds as well at the bottom as on the surface when aquatic insects are hatching. One of the peculiarities of its diet is that it specializes in finding small-sized prey, rarely larger than a half-inch (one centimeter). Larvae of mayflies, trichopterae, and chironomides are the foundation of its diet. In our climate, in waters rich with aquatic insects, the grayling rarely attacks larger prey, worms, or small fish, whereas in the north, in Scotland or in Scandinavia, it is the custom to fish for this species with a large worm, minnow, or spinner.

The grayling, which spawns at the end of April and beginning of May, is a very active feeder in winter. Even when it snows, it feeds on flies at the surface.

At the turn of the century, according to Boisset and Vibert, the grayling was present in many streams in the Ardennes, Lorraine, the Vosges, Alsace, the Franche-Comté, Savoy, Dauphine, and Auvergne-Limousin. In 1958, Vivier identified them only in the Ain, the Doubs, the Loue, the upper Rhone, the Arve, the Isere, the upper Loire, the Allier, the Dore, the Alagnon, and some tributaries of these rivers. Throughout the 1960s populations of graylings decreased somewhat throughout France, victims of pollution and the destruction of their habitat. It was necessary to wait until the end of the 1970s for this trend to be reversed with acclimation tests in various rivers: the Dordogne, upper Seine, Marne, and the Huisne. The infatuation this species inspires in fly fishermen is today the best insurance for its protection and survival. In North America, Arctic grayling live in lakes and rivers and are actively sought in Alaska, the Yukon Territory, and the Northwest Territories.

Its characteristic pupil in the form of a pear pointing forward enables the grayling to quickly identify prey on the surface.

The Atlantic Salmon: royal fish

Although it has become increasingly rare in many rivers, *Salmo salar* continues to exercise a real fascination for fishermen. A royal fish before the Revolution, it remains the king of freshwater fish, the only one worthy of being fished for by the elite of this world.

". . . it remains the king of freshwater fish . . ."

An old English lord, former minister of Queen Victoria, wrote in his memoirs: "Because of my family's position, I experienced the best receptions and the most beautiful women. I had a team of foxes and I rode to the hounds marvelously. I hunted tiger in the Indies and grouse in Scotland, but I never felt as much pleasure as when I was holding a salmon at the end of my line."

Fishing for salmon in a river is different from that of all other species, because it involves a fish that does not feed in freshwater. Returning to the river where they were born, salmon persist in fasting, getting their energy from the fantastic reserves of fats and proteins they accumulate during their ocean sojourn. Never has the expression "to live on love and fresh water" been better applied than to this noble animal, which, after two or three years spent in the cold waters of the glacial Arctic Ocean gorging on krill, herring, and sprats, returns infallibly to the river in which it was born to procreate and then to die there.

". . . to live on love and fresh water . . ."

Thus, when a salmon seizes one of our lures or baits between its jaws, it is not hunger that motivates it. Rather, to more closely examine this object intruding into its territory, it has no other recourse than to take it into its mouth. Scientists studying the behavior of salmon can invoke reactions of aggressiveness, curiosity, annoyance, and playfulness. But perhaps it is a reminder of the ocean banquets to which it was accustomed off the coast of Greenland, and which in one or two years enabled it to grow from a small salmon only slightly larger than a sardine to a fully grown salmon capable of weighing more than 20 pounds.

Male Atlantic salmon weighing more than 30 pounds, caught in Finland.

On Scottish rivers, here the Tay, ghillies are experts in handling large nets.

On the rivers of Iceland, in crystalline waters, fishing is often done by sight with handheld rods.

Above: Surging from the foam, this salmon is trying to cross a waterfall to continue its voyage toward the spawning areas upstream.

Opposite: Prestige and tradition. This large male salmon was caught according to the rules of the art: split bamboo Leonard rod, Vom Hoff reel, and classic "fully dressed" flies.

Under the Romanesque porch of the cathedral of Sainte-Marie in Oloron, salmon fishermen hold a place of honor in the middle of the frieze showing earthly occupations.

In the 19th century, aristocrats and captains of industry paid fortunes to cast a fly in the rivers of Scotland, Norway, and Canada. On the Restigouche River in Quebec, the Million Dollar Pool, at the confluence of this river and the Matapédia, was actually purchased for such a sum in 1890 by the most famous fishing club in New York. Rumor had it at the time, in the salons of Boston and Washington, that it was much easier to be elected to Congress than to obtain an invitation to fish at the Restigouche Salmon Club. In our day, fly-fishing for this fish is considered both an art and a sport without equal, to which the wellborn or rich devote themselves in Anglo-Saxon countries. Tradition is everything! Because, whether in Normandy, Brittany, or the mountain streams of the Oloron—where fishing for salmon is practiced more democratically by casting, using spinners, or even earthworms—in the rivers of the Highlands, Quebec, or New Brunswick, there is no question of casting anything but a fly to tempt so royal a fish.

In England, during the reign of Queen Victoria and the time of splendor for the British Empire, fly-fishing for salmon, and fly tying in

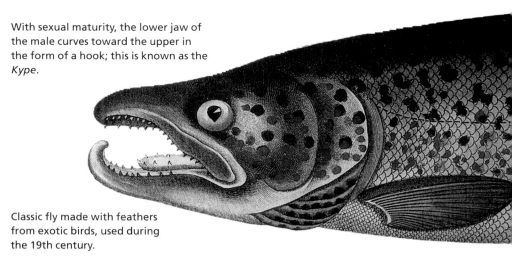

With sexual maturity, the lower jaw of the male curves toward the upper in the form of a hook; this is known as the *Kype*.

Toward the end of autumn, during the spawning period, males and females exhibit the colors of dead leaves.

Classic fly made with feathers from exotic birds, used during the 19th century.

Below and at the bottom: two models of modern flies.

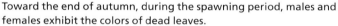

"It was so beautiful that the salmon even jumped out of the river to swallow it."

particular, reached its apogee. Labor was cheap and the materials (feathers of all colors from exotic birds) were brought back from the Indies or the African colonies in the trunks of officers of Her Very Gracious Majesty. In 1895, Major Kelson published his voluminous and magnificent treatise on the tying of salmon flies, which described no fewer than 371 models. This author lived, moreover, until the end of his days with the secret hope of creating, based on knowledgeable arrangements and mixtures of feathers, tinsel, and colored wires, the "exact fly" that no salmon would be able to resist. An old Scottish legend had it that such a fly did exist. It was so beautiful that the salmon even jumped out of the river to swallow it. But because he failed to note the exact proportions of the various silk lines and feathers arranged on the hook, its creator could never replicate it after a particularly large salmon broke the line and carried it off to the bottom of the river.

Splendid specimen of a sea trout from the Morrum River in Sweden.

The Sea Trout: queen of the night

In the rivers of Lapland, during the short Arctic summer, sea trout bite even during the midnight sun.

Whereas in many coastal bodies of water in Brittany, Normandy, Artois, and Picardy, as well as in Béarn and the Basque country, runs of sea trout are still rather abundant, in France there is no real tradition of fishing for this splendid fish, as there is in the British Isles and the Scandinavian countries. There is good reason for this: the prohibition made by the Rural Code against fishing at night, which strongly reduces the possibilities of catching the most nocturnal of salmonids.

In fact, sea trout fear daylight, especially if the waters are clear. In summer, in shallow waters, they hide during the day in the deepest pools, in the shelter of cut-banks or in the grass. There they remain hidden until sunset. It is only when night arrives—and the darker it is without moonlight, the better—that they return to the currents to hunt insects and small fish. Unlike salmon, which don't feed once they have returned to freshwater, sea trout remain rather active in rivers and continue to feed there. On the coasts of Europe (France, Scotland, Ireland, Wales, Scandinavia), the largest runs take place in summer, between the months of June and September. In the rivers of the

The rivers of southern Sweden experience excellent runs of sea trout.

Above: The convex rear edge of the caudal fin makes it possible to differentiate a sea trout from a salmon.

Southern Hemisphere where they have been introduced, in Chile, in Argentina, in New Zealand, it's in January, February, and March, during the southern summer, that the future parents return to freshwater. Spawning in these latitudes takes place in July to August. Sea trout were introduced to North America in 1958; they have earned a reputation as excellent game fish.

Fly-fishing in the dark is agonizing but terribly captivating. At the touch, the line is generally pulled from the fingers, and while the click of the reel sounds and the spool unwinds, you hear the fish splash in the darkness as it leaps out of the water and fights like a devil on the surface, while all the time you are wondering if it has returned to the head of the pool or if its wild course has led it downstream. As it comes to the net, on a fine line and a small wet fly, a sea trout of more than 3 pounds that has just arrived from the ocean is a magnificent catch. When we know that in European waters these fish reach double, even triple, this weight, we understand why British and Scandinavian fishermen hold this fish in greater esteem than the salmon.

Opposite: Sea trout in the rivers of Tierra del Fuego are acrobatic adversaries. It is in the darkness of the night that sea trout bite most boldly.

to your rods!

Steelhead estimated at 22 pounds (10 kilos), caught on the Thompson River in British Columbia.

The Steelhead Trout

On the two shores of the immense Pacific Ocean, from southern California to Alaska on the American coast and from the Sino-Russian border to the north of Kamtchatka on the continent of Asia, the waters contain one of the most fantastic of all sport fish: the steelhead trout.

For ichthyologists, these fish are simply migratory forms of the rainbow trout, which, like salmon, seek more abundant food in the ocean. When they return after one to three years of roaming in the ocean to the rivers where they were born, they are the most beautiful and aggressive adversaries that a fly fisherman can dream of. Their sides are like gleaming blocks of silver punctuated by black crosses, and their backs and their heads are the intense blue-green color of a casting of steel that has barely cooled.

"Their sides are like gleaming blocks of silver punctuated by black crosses . . ."

Their oceanic migrations, like those of salmon, cover great distances, ranging as far as several thousand miles from the mouth of the river where they were born. Tagged in Oregon, one steelhead was caught by a Japanese boat in the middle of the North Pacific, more than three thousand miles (5,000 kilometers) from the place where it was released. Remember that European sea trout practice internal navigation on the coasts of the English Channel, the North Sea, and the Baltic Sea. River migrations may also cover enormous distances, since in some rivers in the American West, the steelheads returned before the construction of dams, at the turn of the century, more than a thousand miles (1,600 kilometers) from the ocean.

"River migrations may also cover enormous distances . . ."

In the United States and Canada, fly-fishing for these fish is considered the queen of freshwater fishing, the equal to that of salmon fishing in Europe. But fishermen who have had the opportunity to catch both species will tell you that comparing the fight of a steelhead to that of an Atlantic salmon is like comparing driving a Porsche on a mountain road with a Mercedes on a highway.

A splendid specimen of a steelhead trout from the Umpqua River in Oregon. Like all wild fish in this river, it will have to be released.

Imitation stone fly, effective in summer.

TROUT FISHING IN AMERICA
Richard Brautigan

"As a child when did I first hear about trout fishing in America? From whom? I guess it was a stepfather of mine.
Summer of 1942.
The old drunk told me about trout fishing. When he could talk, he had a way of describing trout as if they were a precious and intelligent metal.
Silver is not a good adjective to describe what I felt when he told me about trout fishing.
I'd like to get it right.
Maybe trout steel. Steel made from trout. The clear snow-filled river acting as foundry and heat.
Imagine Pittsburgh.
A steel that comes from trout, used to make buildings, trains and tunnels.
The Andrew Carnegie of Trout!"

Above: Simple and reliable, the Saint John by Hardy is one of the best reels.
Opposite: This steelhead is measured before being released.

Like all of our trout, steelhead will go for nymphs.

When it lets loose

. . . the attack is blazing . . .

Pike: spiked teeth and camouflage dress

Vincent Lalu, probably one of the best European pike specialists, here with an 18-pounder caught with a popper.

T he pike is the freshwater shark; it rules there in devastating tyranny like the shark in the middle of the sea. Insatiable in its appetite, it lays waste to fishponds and pools with frightening rapidity.

Perhaps because of this frightening portrait that official science, under the pen of the Count de Lacépède, painted of it in the 18th century, the pike today is still the most sought after carnivore in our waters, the trophy fish par excellence, the one whose preserved head is hung over the mantel of the living room fireplace. It greatly excites the imagination of fishermen, but in addition to its formidably armed voracious mouth, pike can reach a very large size in our waters. The current record in France for line fishing is a fish of 54 pounds (24.50 kilos). Much larger specimens have been taken by commercial fishermen in their nets or during the emptying of ponds. The largest European pikes were caught in Ireland, where the mild and temperate climate, along with the rich lochs with their chalky bottoms, make enormous growth rates possible. But with the help of whiskey and pints of Guinness, these pike must grow even faster after they've been caught.

. . . and it rarely misses its prey.

A pike completely surprised by the taste of a Rapala!

In high season, lures floated on the grass are remarkably efficient.

For pike, red and white plugs always work well.

In 1832, a gardener killed a pike weighing 92 pounds (42 kilos) with an oar during spawning, in a pool near Portumna Castle. Thirty years later, in 1862, a ghillie named John Naughton captured, using a line this time, a 90.5-pound specimen in the Derg loch. Finally, in 1927, the English fishing magazine *The Field* reported the taking, still in Ireland, near Shannon, of a pike weighing 90 pounds (41 kilos).

Among freshwater fish, the pike has the fastest growth rate, reaching 16 inches (40 centimeters) or more, and weighing 1.5 pounds at the end of its first year, 4 pounds at two years, and then gaining 3 to 4 pounds per year. In rivers rich in food fish, weights of 22 pounds (10 kilos) and lengths of 43 inches (1.10 meters) can be reached in seven or eight years. In Sweden and Finland, it should be noted that pike can well tolerate the saltiness of the Baltic Sea and reach colossal sizes by feeding on schools of herring.

Found generally along grassy stretches, hidden by its mottled skin of yellow and brown, the pike lies in wait, perfectly immobile, until its prey passes within its field of view. It then thrusts forward, briskly propelling itself with its dorsal, anal, and caudal fins, using them like the fletching of an arrow at the end of its slender, missilelike body. Its

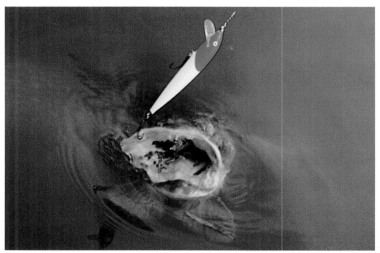

to your rods!

A lure imitating a frog has deceived this suspicious largemouth.

Du Brochet.

Chap. XI.

Ovs mettons le Brochet entre les poiſſons de riuiere, combien qu'il ſe trouue auſſi bien aux palus, é eſtangs, é lacs qu'aux riuieres. Il eſt donc commun à toutes eaux douces. Il n'eſt aucunement poiſſon marin, é ne le trouue l'ō point aux bouches de riuiere, ſyt aux eſtangs de mer, s'il ni eſt porté par force é violence des vndes.

THE TACKLE BOX
Maurice Genevoix

"Out of the water, the pike opens its large, impressive mouth. It is white and full of shadows, white and red, due to the gills that can be seen at the back. And those teeth! And that bronze hook embedded in the fleshy throat! All of this is unexpected, fantastic, and real at the same time: one would think it was a frenetic dream, this calm, this hard, dominant balance. Najard speaks, adding a few brief words of advice: 'Put the net into the water ... deeper, so it doesn't see it.... When it passes right above, lift it. Watch out, I'm bringing it in....' Hop! Bailleul had stiffened all of his muscles. He was bending over, pulled by the burden, his feet slipping on the clay of the embankment. Will he fall forward and hit his head under the water? Najard, holding his line with one hand, his arms in front of him, in a protective gesture, reaches out towards Bailleul. 'No, no, let it go!' says the boy. Alone, he lifts the beast, an enormous pike writhing in a frenzy at the bottom of the distended net."

". . . the pike is indifferent, attacking anything with scales . . ."

". . . the pike is not the insatiable ogre often described . . ."

large mouth stretched wide and its powerful jaws, armed with more than seven hundred teeth, come into play, rarely missing the shiner, gudgeon, or young carp passing by.

Identified by the first naturalists as the *freshwater shark*, the tyrant of the streams, the ogre of the rivers, the pike is indifferent, attacking anything with scales, hair, or feathers that can fit within its powerful jaws. Although whitefish constitute the foundation of its diet, frogs, shrimp, water rats, and even waterfowl (ducklings, moorhens) find their way into its diet. Nevertheless, although it is a very efficient predator, the pike is not the insatiable ogre often described, and it is far from eating its own weight in fish or other marine animals every day. Thus, three large 1-ounce gudgeons and a large shiner two fingers long are the average daily feast of a "big mouth" 10-pounder. Fishermen now know that it is the lack of chronic appetite on the part of the pike, with the exception of a few rare and fleeting moments of feeding frenzy, that is largely responsible for their returning home empty-handed.

The moment of truth: 47 inches (1.20 meters) of muscle and scales arrives at the surface . . . but the beast is not yet in the bottom of the boat.

No need to go to Canada to catch a large pike. Guy Serralta caught this 35-pound (16-kilo) trout in Draveil.

Above: This record 43-pound (500-kilo) pike was caught in a pool of the Orne River.

Beauty and the beast!

Large articulated Rapala are among the best lures.

Opposite: Two beautiful perch that are no dwarfs!

Above: A small Rapala imitating a cyprinid alevin is one of the best lures for perch.

Plate from *L'Histoire naturelle générale et particulière des poissons* by Mark Elieser Bloch (Berlin 1784).

The Perch: always on the alert!

Unlike the pike, the perch likes company. It lives, hunts, and moves with its fellow creatures of the same size, forming schools that vary in numbers according to the measurements and the age of the subjects: several hundred individuals for small, young perch to a few dozen for beautiful stripers of a pound, and three or four subjects for large humpbacks of more than 2 pounds (1 kilo).

This gregarious behavior is important for fishermen to know, since taking the first perch should make them stay in the same place, until, logically, other members of the group are taken. But wait, catch one and the entire school disappears, or at least stops biting, as if the fish had gotten the word. Whereas the pike hunts by lying in wait, the perch hunts on the move, pursuing the unfortunate small fish until the final kill. In fact, it seems that each member of the group selects and isolates a prey that will be tracked until its capture. It is possible to see, on the calm surface of ponds, small shiners spurting to the surface, followed by the wake made by the dorsal fin of their angry predator. Always on the alert, perch are curious fish, attentive to the smallest of movements, and come to inspect anything that might be a source of food. They are attracted to shiny things, and fishermen have quickly learned to use lures of silver or nickel to catch them. The perch is common in freshwater, provided that the current is moderate. There are few in the torrential and cold waters of certain trout rivers that they dislike. It is the most widely represented carnivorous fish in freshwater. In rivers, perch remain sheltered from the current. They like sheer banks, marked by crevices, obstructed with grass or dead wood. Piers, dam eddies, mill outlets, and bridge supports that break the current are good positions. In a pond, they can be found near the sluice gate or along the dike.

Two perfect large humpback perch!

In very low temperatures, perch remain active. In Scandinavia or in Canada, they are caught through the ice.

Ballast, gravel, and sand pits are the biotopes par excellence for pike perch.

The Pike Perch: a menacing eye to see in the shadows!

Originally from Central Europe, introduced in France beginning in 1930, the pike perch only became truly implanted there beginning in the 1960s. In North America, anglers actively pursue a cousin of the pike perch: the esteemed walleye.

". . . pike perch are social fish . . ."

Like practically all of the percids, pike perch are social fish that live and hunt in groups. But unlike perch, who attack their prey on the surface, pike perch are primarily deepwater predators that are particularly fond of the small species of cyprinids: gudgeon, shiners, and bleak. In streams and large rivers, pike perch prefer places where the current is subdued, where the water is calm. Behind obstacles, the ends of islands, large eddies, and backwaters formed by jetties, the deep borders thick with sunken shrubs or dead wood are places for resting and waiting. Hunting grounds are always near these places, but located at the edge of the current. In large, navigable rivers, the first break in the bank that marks the projection before the channel is a first-rate spot. Entrances to

Perca lucioperca

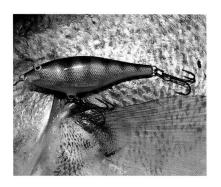

streams and ballast pits that connect with the river are also prime positions. In large bodies of water, especially if the water is clear, the hiding place of the pike perch will depend on two factors: the light and the presence of shelter or obstacles on the bottom. In dark, cloudy weather, pike perch often rise from the lower depths to hunt in less than 3 feet (1 meter) of water. When the sky is blue and the light is bright, they confine themselves to deep water and prefer shady banks. In dammed lakes, submerged trees, sunken hedges, and low retaining walls are positions of ambush for them. In the large ballast pits at the very bottom, it is not always easy to find their hiding places, which vary with the movement of the fish on which they feed.

". . . pike perch often rise from the lower depths to hunt in less than 3 feet (1 meter) of water."

Perca lucioperca

Perca lucioperca

Artificial lakes choked with submerged vegetation are excellent biotopes for black bass.

Don't hesitate to use large streamers to get a black bass to bite.

Most fly-fishing techniques work perfectly for black bass.

100

The Largemouth Bass: an acrobatic fighter

Above: In France, the largemouth bass, unfortunately, rarely exceeds 2 pounds (1 kilo).

The largemouth bass, a fish indigenous to North America, has been introduced to other parts of the world including Europe. At the beginning of the 1960s, on the occasion of a fish census, the Ministry of Waters and Forests recognized the presence of the largemouth bass in some forty departments of France.

The species appeared implanted and definitively acclimated to French waters. Today, French anglers are disappointed, since the largemouth bass population has not kept up, even to previous levels, except in a few rivers and streams in the southwest and the center of France. Opportunist in its search for food and eclectic in its diet, the largemouth bass, also known as the black bass, eats anything that swims within reach of its formidable mouth. The young feed on invertebrates (worms, leeches, insect larvae, etc.) and alevins of other species. Adults eat more fish, but do not disdain insects, worms, batrachians (frogs, tritons, salamanders), waterfowl (ducklings, moorhens . . .), or small aquatic mammals (water rats and shrews). Like other carnivorous fish of still waters, largemouth bass do not like water with much current. When they are found in a river or stream, it is always where there is little or no current. Cutoffs, backwaters, and ballast pits connecting with bodies of water are their preferred locations. Of course, lakes, natural or artificial, ponds, canals, and drainage ditches are biotopes of stagnant water that they prefer, provided that they are full of aquatic vegetation.

Above: Its name of *largemouth* is well deserved.

At the end of a line, the largemouth bass fights like the devil, jumping out of the water, shaking its large mouth as soon as it feels the prick of the hook, and trying as soon as it can to take refuge in the grass or any submerged obstacle. It is certainly a rough fighter, whose acrobatic defense is one of the reasons it is so sought after by sport fishermen. In North America, the largemouth bass is the object of many tournaments and fishing derbies.

Poppers are very noisy surface lures that excite the aggressiveness of the largemouth bass.

Albert Drachkovitch, the master of ten thousand carp.

The Carp: a quiet force

Beyond the phenomenon of current fashion, there has always been a tradition of carp fishing in France, especially in rural areas. Each region, each local area, used to have its preferred bait: potatoes in the Loire, chestnuts in Limousin, broad beans in the Saône . . .

". . . the carp was the largest of France's strictly freshwater fish . . ."

For centuries and before the recent acclimation of catfish in French rivers, the carp was the largest of France's strictly freshwater fish, and thus the trophy par excellence for fishermen. The record for France, and for the world, for a carp taken for sport was a specimen caught in 1981 in the Yonne that tipped the scales at 81.5 pounds (37 kilos). The fever of current carp fishermen is motivated in part by the hope of beating this record, since the discovery of giant carp in Saint Cassien Lake, in the Var, in the Der-Chantecoq reservoir, in Lorraine, and most recently in a Roumanian lake where "grannies" of more than 88 pounds (40 kilos) swim alongside catfish of 110 pounds (50 kilos). Reaching enormous size, the carp is moreover a fish that fights valiantly at the end of the line. This is particularly true of carp in France's large rivers, such as the Loire and the Rhône, where they are accustomed to fighting against the current. Compared with heavy fish that move sluggishly at the bottom of ponds, dam lakes, and canals, river carp are real bluebloods whose fight at the end of the line is equal to that of a salmon. The carp has also always attracted fishermen because it is considered clever, defiant, even "intelligent," and thus difficult to make bite. Instinctively prudent, the carp in fact learns to be wary of the traps that are set for it. This is even more true today, when 90 percent of the carp that are caught are released (no-kill fishing) and have learned their lesson. And this is what motivates modern carp fishermen: the need to trick an adversary that is smart and has learned to elude traps it has seen before.

". . . it is considered clever, defiant . . ."

A carp fisherman's camp: strings of bobbers, electronic bite sensors, and reels.

102

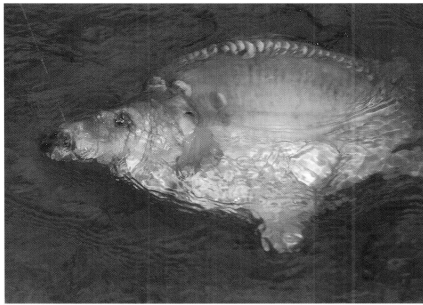

A large humpback "mirror" carp comes up to the net.

In large bodies of water, carp fishermen can cast more than 85 yards (80 meters).

The bar, a fish of the foam, likes water that is stirred up and well oxygenated.

These "cigars" with propellers are among the best lures for bar.

Bar or Loup: one of the most voracious fish

It was the Romans, great lovers of fish, who called it *lupus* (wolf) because of its voracity and its habit of hunting in packs. This king of our saltwater fish owes its reputation as much to its valiant fight and the sporting qualities required to fish for it as to the excellence of its flesh at the dinner table.

". . . it has as many names as the shores it frequents."

Bar in the English Channel and the Atlantic, loup in the Mediterranean—it has as many names as the shores it frequents. *Drenek* in Brittany, it is called *louvine* in the Vendée and *loubine* on the Landais coast. Bar frequent the European shores of the Atlantic from the latitude of southern Scotland as far as Agadir, in Morocco. It is also present in the Mediterranean and the Adriatic, and on both sides of the Bosphorus, in a small portion of the Black Sea. A coastal fish that hunts in the bottom vegetation, in the foam that breaks at the bottom of cliffs or masses of fallen rock, it returns with the onset of winter to the deeper and warmer waters of the sea. But for sustenance, it always returns to the coast, according to the rhythm of the tides that stir up, mix, move, uncover, and displace an entire microcosm of worms, shrimp, crab, small fish, and mollusks that hide in the sand, under the algae, and in rock crevices. The adult diet is more eclectic and varied according to season and available prey. It ranges from sand fleas, which bar know how to find at high tide in decomposing wrack, to saltwater fish that they hunt in the open sea. In summer and in autumn, they eat small fish: sprats, sardines, and sand eels, which they round up and drive back into the bay. Sand worms, crustaceans (soft- and hard-shell crabs), and mollusks (cuttlefish, squid, small octopus) play an important part in their diet. They are extremely voracious: everything seems suited to their insatiable appetites, and there have even been cases when, after a storm has pulled them out of their nest, young seabirds (gulls, petrels) have been found in the stomachs of large bar caught at the foot of Breton cliffs.

" . . . everything seems suited to their insatiable appetites . . ."

That's where they hunt, in the breakers beyond the third wave.

The Rattlin Rap, a noisy lure that is formidable in its efficiency on French coasts.

The large propellers of the Big-Big noisily stir up the water and excite the bar's hunting instinct.

Two "small" bluefin tuna of about 225 pounds (100 kilos) suspended from the weighing crossbar at La Grande-Motte.

The Bluefin Tuna: an endangered giant

I ts name comes from the Greek *thunnes*, which means "quick start." For many, this magnificent fish, which Aristotle treated in his "History of Animals" as one of the marvels of nature represents an enigma for scientists.

"The bluefin tuna is the largest of all tuna . . ."

Although the species, pursued by commercial fishermen, is close to extinction, we have not yet deciphered all the secrets of its fantastic migrations. The bluefin tuna is the largest of all tuna and one of the largest bony fish in the ocean. The current sport fishing record for a fish caught with rod and reel is 1,496 pounds, or 679 kilos, which is not too far from the record in all categories of marlin, which is 1,560 pounds. There is no doubt that in the waters off Sicily, Spain, and North Africa, bluefin tuna weighing close to a ton have been caught.

These indefatigable sea voyagers, who can live at least thirty-five years, pass alternately during their gigantic migrations from one coast of the Atlantic to the other, searching for food or spawning grounds. Tuna tagged off the coast of Florida have been caught in the seas off Norway sometimes less than two months later. Pierre Clostermann, who has fished for them in all oceans, compares these fish to giant biceps that swim . . . and this is exactly what they are. Veritable muscular torpedoes, hydrodynamically perfect, these fish have been clocked at speeds of more than 55 miles (90 kilometers) per hour. Once they take off, anything that's not needed for propulsion or that would cause the slightest drag in the water disappears. The pectoral fins flatten along the body, and the dorsal fin retracts completely into a slot that forms a sheath on top of the back. When faced with a potential enemy, a walrus or shark, their only defense is their phenomenal speed in escaping. And this is what sport fishermen seek, their enormous reels burning from the moment the tuna feels the bite of the hook.

". . . these fish have been clocked at speeds of more than 55 miles (90 kilometers) per hour."

MEMORIES AT THE END OF A LINE
Pierre Clostermann

"Today, the problem of the bluefin tuna in the Mediterranean is dramatic. The negligence of the French Ministry of Maritime Affairs, the incompetence of officials who have dealt with this question, the criminal irresponsibility of professionals, the rackets, the unscrupulous Japanese buyers have resulted in the short term in the end of the splendid 'Thunnus tynnus' in our waters. Considered a species in the process of extinction, this fish, which travels from Brazil to the Bouches-du-Rhone, from Labrador to the Bahamas, from the Atlantic coasts of Morocco to Tunisia and the Adriatic, is massacred without restraint or sense of decency by French, Spanish, and Italian professionals."

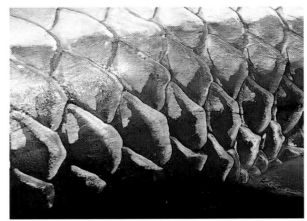

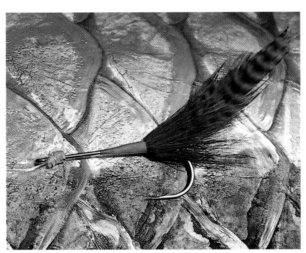

Opposite: Practically all record tarpon of 220 pounds (100 kilos) have been caught in the Sherbro estuary, in Sierra Leone.

On top: Close-up of the scales of a tarpon.

Above: The best flies imitate shrimp, the tarpon's favorite food.

Like a demon escaping from its box, the tarpon explodes on the surface of the sea.

108

The Tarpon: dynamite on the end of the line

Fly-fishing for tarpon is surely one of the most wonderful, and at the same time one of the most difficult, kinds of fishing. Almost as soon as the guide, you will have to spot the large silver features undulating under the mirrored surface of the ocean.

". . . if the tarpon takes the small fly and if your cast has been successful . . ."

Then you will have only a few seconds to cast the fly precisely, ahead of the form, often more than 60 feet (20 meters) and with a wind blowing in the wrong direction. Finally, if the tarpon takes the small fly and if your cast has been successful, be prepared for a battle where you won't get away with a single slip and that you will remember for the rest of your fishing life. It is in fact an insane bet to try to catch, with equipment hardly stronger than that used to fish for large trout or salmon, these true brutes of the ocean, whose average weight is at least ten times greater than that of these species—and especially whose fight at the end of the line is to trout and salmon what a tropical cyclone is to a light breeze on a lake. Hemingway, during his stay in

Fly-fishing for tarpon is a true hunt that takes place in very shallow water.

With a large pole made of carbon fiber, the guide silently pushes the boat on the flats.

In Florida, all tarpon with the exception of possible records, are released after the traditional photo.

Tonight, it is a celebration in the village for these children in Sierra Leone, who will have tarpon on the menu.

A few yards from the boat, the giant desperately shakes its head to get rid of the hook.

At right: The large defeated tarpon is held against the ship's rail to take out the hook and set it free.

"These fish have been seen to jump more than six feet (2 meters) above the waves . . ."

Key West during the 1930s, complained about the number of bamboo rods that the tarpon of the Dry Tortugas (an archipelago off the coast of Key West) had caused to give up the ghost. What remained of his equipment, twisted rods and exploded reels, is today on view, with the yellowing photographs of "Papa," as Hemingway was known, and of his tarpon, on the wall in back of the most famous bar in Key West, Sloppy Joe's.

It's this physical engagement with the tarpon that still excites American sportsmen today. When fly-fishing, the least error, the smallest fault of inattention, is immediately acknowledged by a break at the end of the line, which is generally not more than 12- or 15-pound test. This is, in fact, a real boxing match, and the fisherman, if he wants to emerge the victor, cannot give his adversary one moment of rest. The first minutes of battle with the *silver king*, as tarpon are called in Florida, are a mixture of brute force, primitive savagery, and uncontrolled explosion. These fish have been seen to jump more than 6 feet (2 meters) above the waves, and every year, in the Keys, it happens that a tarpon that has been hooked falls during its aerial acrobatics into the fisherman's boat. Since the skiffs used for fishing these fish are very flat, low in the water, and not more than 15 feet in length, there is not enough room for everybody! There is only one thing left for the guide and his client to do: jump into the water and leave the boat to the tarpon while waiting for it to become calm, after it has destroyed all the superstructure of the small boat. But as violent and spectacular as it is during the first few minutes, the battle with a giant tarpon can then be transformed into a test of endurance that can last more than three, four, five, or six hours. The fisherman rarely emerges as the victor. Billy Pate, who held the majority of world records for tarpon caught on flies, recalls that his current record of 188 pounds required ten hours of effort before it could be hauled into the boat. Under the implacable Florida sun, Billy lost more than

10 pounds (5 kilos), and for three hours he could not open the fingers of his right hand, so tightly were they clenched around the handle of his rod. Another time, he fought a giant tarpon, estimated at more than 200 pounds, for twelve hours, before losing it when gaffing because the defeated fish was attacked by a gigantic hammerhead shark as long, he recalls, as the small boat from which he was fishing. The tarpon had led them into the vicinity of the Gulf Stream, and a Coast Guard cutter located them after nightfall.

Many fishermen who have defeated the largest tuna and giant marlin off the coast of the Great Barrier Reef in Australia are unanimous in declaring that taking a tarpon of more than 150 pounds with a fly rod is the supreme challenge for a real sport fisherman.

These flies, which imitate small mullets, are a sure bet.

On the immense flats, fly-fishing for bonefish or permits is a challenge.

The gigantic eye of the permit enables it to outsmart most of the lures that it is offered.

Supreme reward: Taking a permit with a fly rod on the flats.

The Bonefish and the Permit: getting them to bite is an art

In places where they are fished, such as Florida or the Bahamas, the bonefish and the permit are certainly the most difficult fish to get to bite in any ocean.

". . . impossible to catch by fly-fishing . . ."

In the Keys, between Miami and Key West, where for more than a quarter of a century "catch and release" has been systematically practiced for these species, these fish, already among the most defiant, always on the alert, have become almost impossible to catch by fly-fishing. Their gregarious behavior means that in a group of ten individuals, one being frightened because it recognizes as suspect the impact of the line or the plop of the fly on the water means that in the next second, the entire school literally "explodes" and flees as fast as their fins will move them.

But even though the hardest thing is making them bite, conducting the battle and winning is also no foregone conclusion, so great are their power and their swimming speed. The bonefish and the permit are the sole coastal fish whose takeoff and speed can be compared to those of the largest predatory fish such as tuna and marlins. But unlike the latter, their crazy course takes place not in deep water, but in the flats, those immense expanses of coral sand covered at high tide with just enough water to hide their backs. It's common in these shallows for a large permit to travel more than a mile nonstop, while the guide's boat, its motor in gear, follows it closely, and for the fisherman, line extended to the breaking point, to give the fish not a moment's respite as he relentlessly tries not to stop its escape, but at least to throw its swimming off balance.

". . . the trophy fish par excellence . . ."

For American fly fishermen, these two fish, although they do not reach heavy weights—6 to 9 pounds (3 to 4 kilos) on the average for the bonefish and double for the permit—are nevertheless considered the trophy fish par excellence, those whose capture owes everything to the fisherman's skill, knowledge, and will to win.

This nursing shark is inoffensive, but other species hunt permits and bonefish.

The permit's enormous caudal fin, deeply cut in the shape of a *V*, indicates a swimmer of fantastic speed.

The Sailfish: a terrible adversary

Easily recognizable by its enormous dorsal fin in the form of a sail or flag, cobalt blue with crimson glints, the sailfish is the most widespread rostrum fish (marlin family) in the tropical waters of the entire world. Because of their aggressiveness and their natural tendency to hunt small prey on the surface, sailfish are the dream targets for saltwater fishermen using light lines.

The large, brilliantly colored "plumage" excites the sailfish's aggressiveness.

The category of 30-pound lines should be reserved for beginners. Lines of 12 to 20 pounds test are the best ones for these fantastic high-speed fighters to express themselves for the great pleasure of the fisherman and possible spectators. Off the coast of Dakar, every summer beginning in the month of June, but especially in July, August, and September, fantastic concentrations of these fish come together. It is not unusual, on a lucky day, to hook twenty of these magnificent fighters, which, during the first few minutes of the battle, spend more time in the air than in the water. The strike is almost

From left to right: En route to the fishing areas.
The sailfish dances above the waves.
Fly-fishing for rostrum fish requires teamwork.
At the end of the battle . . . the sailfish, played out, will be seized by the rostrum before being released.

always preceded by a chase by the predator behind the bait or the lure that flaps on the surface in the wake of the boat. The sailfish madly thrashes, trying to "kill" the bait, which continues its course on the waves. This merry-go-round, one of the most beautiful and exciting spectacles that a fisherman may be privileged to see, takes place over the course of several minutes, the large fish making its sail click by folding and unfolding it like an enormous wet fan several times in succession on the surface of the blue waters before deciding to swallow the bait. On the Pacific coast of Mexico, Panama, and Costa Rica, where these fish are not only abundant, but much larger than their Atlantic cousins, it is possible, after having teased them and lured them to the stern of the boat using bait with no hooks, to make them bite using a fly. It's a good idea to have at least 350 yards of reserve backing on the reel. When they are hooked on the edge of the rostrum or in the bony part of the jaw and not in the stomach, as is most often the case in conventional fishing, their fight increases tenfold. They launch into a veritable aerial ballet, offering fishermen moments they will never forget.

In Quepos, on the Pacific coast of Costa Rica, the sun sets almost all year long on an ocean as calm as a lake.

115

While one of the
assistants holds the
end of the line tightly,
the other tags the fish,
which will then
immediately be freed.

The Marlin: the fisherman's dream

Alongside the boat,
ready to be freed, all
the fury of the king of
the oceans can be
read in the eye of this
blue marlin from the
Caribbean.

"We thus see, joined together in the makaira, the size, the speed, the skill, the weapons, the vigor, everything that can give it the authority and even enable it to exercise a terrible tyranny on the weak inhabitants of the ocean." Lacépède (Natural History of Fish)

"…these two species are the giants of the rostrum fish…"

On the basis of a drawing of a 365-pound specimen that washed up after a powerful storm on a beach near the Ile de Ré in 1802, Lacépède described the blue marlin. The notes of the subprefect of La Rochelle indicated the fish's coloration as "blackish," so the illustrious savant gave the name *Makaira nigricans* for scientific posterity to the blue marlin, whose color actually turns black after death. Nevertheless, the true "black knight of the seas" (*makaira* in Gaelic means "knight") does exist, but in other oceans, the Indian and the Pacific. The black marlin (*Makaira indica*) described by Cuvier in 1832 scours the vast expanses of these oceans, from the eastern coasts of Africa to those of Central America and Peru, passing by Indonesia, Australia, and all the other islands in the intertropical zones of the Pacific. But to make

116

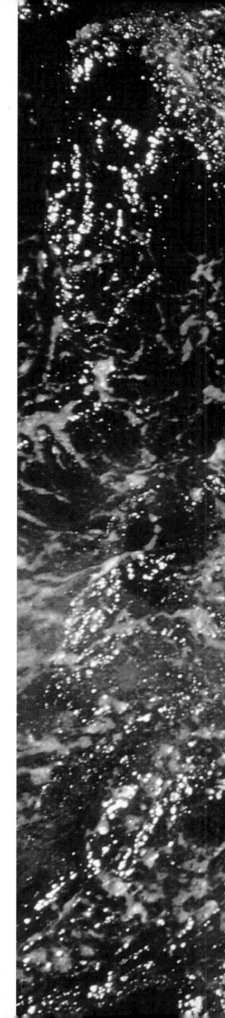

to your rods!

Sharpened like the rapier of a swordsman, the rostrum of this small white marlin is a formidable weapon.

Rods and reels of 130 pounds for fishing giant marlin.

ISLANDS IN THE STREAM
Ernest Hemingway

"The fish came in closer, appearing as long and as wide as a large tree trunk in the water. David watched it and glanced at the end of his rod to be sure the line was not becoming tangled. For the first time in six hours, his back, his arms and his knees were no longer experiencing traction, and Thomas Hudson saw the muscles of his knees shake and tremble. Eddy was bent over the side with the gaff and Roger was pulling slowly and without jerking. 'It weighs more than five hundred kilos,' said Eddy. (Then he added very calmly:) 'Roger, the hook is only holding on by one line.' 'Can you reach it?' asked Roger. 'Not yet,' said Eddy. 'Continue to come in closer, gently, gently.'"

"These two species are the most sought after…"

"…the large pectoral fins of the black marlin are rigid…"

things even more complicated, the blue marlin, the one called *nigricans* by Lacépède, is also found in the Indian and Pacific Oceans. Although these two species are the giants of the rostrum fish, and can easily exceed weights of 1,100 pounds (500 kilos), they are distinguished, in addition to their different colorations when they are alive, by the fact that the large pectoral fins of the black marlin are rigid and cannot be folded along the length of the body as is the case with the blue marlin.

Whether they are blue or black, the marlins of the Atlantic, the Indian, and Pacific Oceans exercise a veritable fascination for game fishermen. These two species are the most sought after, at great expense, by the skippers and crews of Bertram, Hatteras, and other floating war machines, capable of speeds of five to six knots, in raging seas, so that the fisherman in his combat seat remains in contact with the fish. What a sight to see these ocean heavyweights behind the boat, sometimes less than ten yards from the beach, suddenly project themselves above the surface, or take off by sculling on their tails to begin a 400 yard sprint across the waves, three-quarters of their body out of the water, while the drag of the reel screams. These fish have been scientifically clocked at more than 37 miles (60 kilometers) per

hour, a speed they can maintain for several hundred yards. That makes them, along with the tuna, among the most rapid fish in the ocean. They are also the most hardy. Many "big game" fishermen have had the bitter experience of losing a marlin, and some have even had somebody take over for them in the battle seat for several—sometimes more than ten—hours, before being obliged to admit defeat and cut the line at nightfall. For all of these reasons, blue and black marlins are considered the most fantastic adversaries on lines of 80 or 130 pounds, the maximum resistance authorized by the rules of big game sport fishing.

In the category of middleweights, the striped marlin is also a splendid and acrobatic fighter, provided that lighter lines are used, with a maximum test of 30 to 50 pounds. Among striped marlin, record fish may exceed 440 pounds (200 kilos) in weight. Finally, in the category of featherweights, the white marlin, which rarely exceeds 110 pounds (50 kilos), is fun to fish for on very fine line, even fly line, as is done more and more often.

"... record fish may exceed 440 pounds (200 kilos) in weight."

PHOTO CREDITS

All photographs are by Pierre Affre or from his private collection, except for: Bernard Dufour,
pages 74–75, pages 116–119; ING/Copyright, pages 34–37.

PHOTO CAPTIONS FOR INTRODUCTORY PAGES

Pages 6–7: Salmon fishing tackle from the start of the 20th century;
pages 20–21: Charles Ritz giving a casting demonstration on the man-made lake in the Bois de Boulogne;
pages 40–41: On the Rynda River in the Kola Peninsula;
pages 74–75: Blue marlin in all its glory.

LITERARY QUOTATIONS

Richard Brautigan, *Trout Fishing in America*, C. Bourgeois, 1974.
Pierre Clostermann, *Memories at the End of a Fishing Line*, Arthaud, 1994.
Maurice Genevoix, *The Tackle Box*, Grasset, 1983.
Ernest Hemingway, *The Old Man and the Sea*, Gallimard, 1996.
Ernest Hemingway, *Islands in the Stream*, Gallimard, 1971.

Conceived and produced by Copyright SA.
Graphic design: Ute-Charlotte Hettler
Layout: Odile Delaporte
Cover: Ute-Charlotte Hettler and Claire Brenier
Editorial coordination: Isabelle Raimond

First edition for the United States and Canada published by Barron's Educational Series, Inc., 2001.
American edition copyright (c) 2001 by Barron's Educational Series, Inc.
Original title in French: *la vie rêvée du Pêcheur*
© 1999 Copyright SA, Paris, France

All inquiries should de addressed to:
Barron's Educational Series, Inc.
250 Wireless Boulevard
Hauppauge, New York 11788
http://www.barronseduc.com

Library of Congress Catalog Card No. 00-106387

International Standard Book No. 0-7641-5316-1
Printed in Spain

9 8 7 6 5 4 3 2 1